HAPPY FOOD

FOR LIFE

Niklas Ekstedt

& Henrik Ennart

Photography: David Loftus

Design and Illustration: Katy Kimbell

HAPPY FOOD

FOR LIFE

HEALTH, FOOD & HAPPINESS

BLOOMSBURY ABSOLUTE

LONDON · OXFORD · NEW YORK · NEW DELHI · SYDNEY

CONTENTS

PART 1. YOU'RE AS HEALTHY AS YOUR PLANET

PART 2. MEALS THAT CHEER

Foreword

The evidence is piling up. The meals we eat affect how well both we and our planet are!

People who eat Western junk food without fibre-rich vegetables, but with lots of meat and fast carbohydrates, are more often mentally unwell. And such food makes the planet sick, too. Conversely, varied food cooked from fresh ingredients with lots of fibre-rich vegetables and whole grains increases our chances of feeling healthy, full of energy and satisfied with life.

Fortunately, food that feeds the soul for exactly this reason also turns out to be best for the environment, the climate, biological diversity, a sustainable food supply, animal welfare and – not least – your heart and the rest of your body.

It's a classic win-win situation, and we haven't even mentioned that it tastes really good too.

Perhaps this all sounds obvious, but despite a global epidemic of mental illness, the central role that food and the gut play in this has thus far been completely eclipsed by pills.

In recent decades, cardiovascular disease, certain sorts of cancer, diabetes and dementia have been linked to poor diet, a lack of physical activity and general lifestyle choices. Initially, these new ideas have always encountered resistance. Now history is repeating itself.

This book is for anyone who's begun to understand that body and brain are linked, and that food and gut flora are crucial to both. For anyone who wants to keep up with an ongoing scientific paradigm shift.

A number of the discoveries that we will talk about in this book have never previously received attention outside a very narrow group of researchers. And yet these are discoveries that should give rise to debate and which will affect the entire human race. We feel a bit like whistleblowers.

The book is also for anyone who's thinking, 'Well, what on earth do I do now? On a normal, busy day, in the kitchen surrounded by hungry children?'

We want to focus on the very latest dietary knowledge and give you the tools to transform it into delicious meals through lots of practical recipes. We'll also be discussing a range of ingredients, and Niklas will reveal how he finally succeeded in getting his reluctant children to eat healthily. Well ... sometimes, at least.

We've said it before, but it's worth repeating. Your large intestine, or colon, is like a tank reactor, where the contents ferment and simmer. It produces all the different types of hormone and signal substances that control your emotions. It's really no coincidence that the gut is sometimes called 'the second brain'.

Food regulates how we feel, and it does so here and now. Within 24 hours, the food you eat will have started to alter the flora of bacteria that live in your guts in a way that it's now possible to measure. Because you really are what you eat. And more often than you think, you feel how you eat too.

Thanks to new DNA techniques, investigation of our gut flora is progressing at amazing speed.

Since our previous book, *Happy Food*, which was published in Sweden in 2017, more than 10,000 new research studies have been published about how our bacteria affect us at the deepest level. This means that an entire quarter of all the knowledge about this area is only a few months old. Two out of three studies are at most three years old.

We're living through a knowledge explosion. The image that's emerging shows how the stomach, immune system, brain and our mental well-being form a cohesive whole.

If such a simple thing as the food on our plates can contribute to epidemics of obesity, diabetes, chronic bowel diseases, gluten intolerance, asthma and food allergies, there's no time to lose.

All of these cases, and many more besides, involve conditions that are linked to chronic inflammation and an increased risk of anxiety and depression. We can no longer separate what goes on in the brain from what goes on in the body. What's usually called co-morbidity – where someone has one or more conditions in addition to a primary condition – is more the rule than the exception.

Sometimes this begins in the mind, perhaps through experiences that the person has gone through, and spreads to the rest of the body because the immune system is affected. In other cases, it begins in the body. Many of the diseases and conditions that are becoming increasingly common begin with an infection.

The researchers we interviewed constantly return to the immune system and how it is weakened. And where is the immune system located? Today, researchers agree that 70–80% of it is located in the gut. This means that your stomach's mood has consequences for your entire body.

Many things affect your gut environment and its inhabitants, and thus your ability to resist disease. These include stress, poor sleep and medicines, but the most important is the food on your plate. Researchers are still only at the early stage of understanding the connection, but it's already clear that food is one of the things that can really help us to stay healthy and give us vital energy.

Even long ago, Hippocrates, often viewed as the father of modern medicine, stated that there was a clear connection between the stomach and mental well-being. You only need to have a brief dose of gastroenteritis to realise that what goes on in the stomach can create a state of acute anxiety. This is an inherited feeling stimulated by our own immune system to encourage us to hide away, gather our strength and avoid infecting other people.

Our emotions rarely arise by chance – instead, they have a clear function.

The bacteria in your gut even seem to contribute to sugar cravings. When you eat a lot of sweet things, for example, bacteria thrive that then start to produce dopamine. This means that you soon begin to associate sweet things with happiness and well-being.

In our previous book, *Happy Food*, we depicted the cutting edge and fast-moving research relating to our gut flora and what's known as the gut-brain axis.

In *Happy Food For Life*, which you're now reading, we explore that connection in greater depth. In Part 1, we peer in wonder into the future, part fascinated, part terrified of what it offers us. In Part 2, we abandon theories and give concrete tips on food preparation and the choice of ingredients.

In a time when artificial intelligence is expected to soon be able to monitor our health, we also want to take a look at our own experiences and mental impressions. A look at the traditional meal time, at how people meet over food and the importance of conscious eating that involves every sense.

If fibre-rich food can contribute to reinforcing our gut flora and our immune system, there are other things that pull in the opposite direction. When the easily digested, fibre-poor junk food is sucked up in the small intestine, the kind microbes further down in the colon are put on a tough starvation diet.

Lots of sugar, refined carbohydrates and poor quality processed fats nourish exactly the sort of aggressive bacteria that can contribute to what's known as a leaky gut, and to chronic inflammation.

We'd also like to hold up a warning sign about the gastroenteritis bacteria that thrive in intensive livestock production, and which seem to contribute to mental illness in a way that has previously gone completely unnoticed. Hello, public health authorities! Do something!

We also interview researchers who warn of additional risks with using too many antibiotics, in addition to those we're already aware of.

Of course, food isn't the only factor underlying good health. Social networks, a feeling of meaningfulness, exercise and a healthy environment are others.

But food is a major and important part of the puzzle that has previously been overlooked.

Our gut flora reflect our surroundings. They force us to think about something other than ourselves. Because without the world around us burgeoning with life and promoting species diversity, we can't have sufficient life force ourselves.

The equation is crystal clear: it's hard to be healthy on a sick planet.

There's always a risk of exaggerated expectations when science opens new doors. Over time, when the dust has settled, the truth can usually be found somewhere between hype and pessimism.

Many researchers suffered from the excessive hype when the human genome was mapped. Twenty years ago, we thought gene technology would solve all our health problems. So this time they'd rather lower expectations. In particular, many researchers want to avoid promoting a probiotics industry that's happy to take its profits in advance.

And don't be so sure that it's always your own needs that have to be satisfied. It can just as well be your microbes demanding more when you're hungry!

So we've deliberately adopted a moderate stance. Because the reality is still fantastic. We aren't primarily interested in capsules containing living bacterial cultures. Like all the other researchers we've spoken to, we want to highlight good, fibre-rich and ideally fermented food that can make both you and your billions of bacteria sated and satisfied. Despite the new findings we present in this book, you should obviously go to the doctor if you're sick.

Lagom is an ancient Swedish word that means neither too much nor too little. Perhaps it comes from before the Viking Age, when food was shared at the communal hearth and people learned to take a share that meant everyone else got some too.

We think that the word *lagom* is an ideal description of what healthy food and a healthy lifestyle means. The key to good health is eating as varied a diet as possible. Not sticking to extreme food habits or body ideals, or stuffing yourself with a few selected superfoods.

Just like life, food is something to enjoy, not to be scared of. It's hard to get too much healthy, well-prepared food. Food isn't primarily a means, it's a goal in itself.

Niklas Ekstedt is one of Sweden's foremost star chefs. His cutting-edge cooking expertise and in-depth knowledge of ingredients and traditional cookery have made it possible to transform the latest scientific findings into exquisite and innovative dishes that everyone can prepare. Niklas is one of the people who introduced ambitious Scandinavian food onto the international stage, and he has taken part in a long list of TV series.

Henrik Ennart is a multi-award winning journalist and author. For the last 15 years, as a science journalist at *Svenska Dagbladet* newspaper, in books and on TV, he has written about food, health and ageing. In several series of articles, he has examined the link between mental illness and chronic inflammation that simmers under the surface for many people. In recent years, Henrik has explored research relating to the gut flora, participating in a number of international scientific conferences on the subject, making several research trips and interviewing leading researchers around the world.

Together, we have written the book *Happy Food For Life*, which contains 50 recipes that are both tasty and healing, not merely for the body but also for the soul.

The secret is that food which creates a sound and multicultural micro-landscape in your gut must be as varied as your gut flora. This is food that's diverse, colourful, tasty, healthy and simple to cook. We call it happy food!

Fact: Microbes

The gut flora consists of various types of micro-organisms, or microbes. These include bacteria, but also fungi, archaea, parasites and lots of viruses, all of which affect each other. The bacteria dominate and are thus far the subject of most research.

YOU'RE AS HEALTHY AS YOUR PLANET

Part 1.

Everything starts in the gut. For every day
that passes, we learn more about our internal
ecosystem, how diet affects us over time, and
how the external environment interacts with
the internal one. Research results stream in
constantly, and here we go through the latest
news about the importance of the gut flora
for our well-being, together with the changes
taking place in how and what we eat. We also
discuss how you can look after your gut flora
in the best possible way. And all followed by
lots of delicious recipes that won't merely
improve your mental well-being, but will
also extend your life!

BOTTOMS UP!

CHAPTER I.

Mathias Dahlgren
Det naturliga köket

An insight that turns everything on its head

There's a lot to think about when it comes to the fantastic discoveries now being made about our gut flora. So at the start of this book, we're going to take a short journey of reflection about our place in the universe: where do we come from? Where are we? Where are we going? But don't panic. We're gradually getting closer to talking about ingredients and Niklas' delicious recipes.

If, like Bertolt Brecht, you consider that food comes before morals, you can start reading the book from the other end. And we'll meet up somewhere in the middle. That works equally well. So let's start!

In the last thousand years, humans have gradually, and often after a great deal of anguish, been forced to adapt to revolutionary ideas, such as the Earth not being the centre of the universe.

Now we're faced with another fact that's just as hard to digest. The new insight that we can no longer claim to be ourselves. There's only a small extent to which I, Henrik, and you, the reader, are independent, separate individuals. Because it turns out that we're actually parts of a personal ecosystem. Or even several.

When I look in the mirror, what I see is only 43% myself. In terms of the number of cells, about half of those we carry around are actually our bacterial flora! The majority of these can be found in the gut, and particularly in the colon. But bacteria also populate the mouth and nose and cover every nook and cranny of the skin.

There are around 40 trillion of them, and every gram of mucus covering the walls of your colon contains billions of bacteria. Together they weigh about 1.4 kilos, which is about the same as your brain. And as if that wasn't enough, our microbes carry up to 99.9% of all of our genetic material, and in many cases they do the work for us.

It's largely microbes that run our digestive processes. They manufacture the vitamins and fatty acids we need, they can produce all the signal substances and hormones our brains use, and it's largely our microbes that break down and extract energy and nutrients from the food we eat.

About a third of all naturally occurring substances that circulate in our bloodstream, and which contribute in various ways to essential biological processes, are manufactured by our microbes.

With only about 23,000 genes in the human genome, we're quite simple constructions. For example, normal winter wheat has five times as many genes.

Instead, our characteristics are largely programmed into our bacterial flora, which together have up to 1,000 times more genomes than us – or up to 20 million genes.

Because a bacterium generally lives for around 12 hours before it splits in two, there are grounds for saying that, at least on a genetically functional level, we wake up as new people every day.

While our own genome is rigid and not pre-disposed to rapid transformation, our microbes give us access to their extreme ability to adapt to the many possible changes in our environment. Researchers will be trying to understand the incredibly complex interplay between our own genes and those of our microbes for many years into the future. But it's already clear that we can borrow countless chemical processes from those microbes – which means our own DNA doesn't need to be able to cope with those processes.

The impact of these bacteria on us is enormous. They contribute to and design everything from our body shape and brain to our digestive system and skeleton. They affect emotions such as hunger, desire and anxiety and contribute to shaping our behaviour and personality.

This is an insight that changes everything. To understand what happens to us on a mental level and how we should feel healthy and full of positive energy, we can no longer merely look right up at the top of the body, in the brain. Many of the answers can instead be found further down, in the stomach.

To this, we must also add the crucial importance of microbes in our immune system, where they can attack unwelcome bacteria and viruses, neutralise toxic substances and act as supervisors for our own immune cells.

This mutual dependency – or symbiosis – isn't actually so surprising. Bacteria existed on Earth for billions of years before us, and on a bacterial cell level give and take are self-evident. Bacteria borrow healthy characteristics from each other, including those essential for life itself, and that's how humans and all other more advanced animals have evolved. They need us and we need them.

In other words, there are plenty of solid reasons for no longer considering ourselves as separate individuals but instead beginning to see ourselves as ecosystems.

Researchers even have a word for it: *holobiont*. This means that humans and their microbes together constitute an organic unit that consists of many different species. A 'multi-species ecological unit'.

Sometimes the stomach is called the second brain, but in evolutionary terms it's rather the reverse that applies. If we look a long way back, humans originated from microbes that weren't much more than a tube: a microscopic digestive tract surrounded by its own nervous system. The brain in the head turned up later, and it was only right at the end of human development that the parts arrived that make independent decision-making possible.

One early brain function for all living beings seems to have been acting as a kind of GPS to find the way back to places where food could usually be found. And of course this must have been a crucial characteristic for survival, which explains why we often have very accurate memory images of places where we ate the best meals of our lives. For example, I'll never forget an incredibly delicious grapefruit that I bought for a few pesos by the roadside in southern Mexico nearly 30 years ago. If I close my eyes, I can still see it all as if it was yesterday.

In this biological predecessor of Google Maps, information is sent from the stomach up to the brain's memory centre via the large vagus nerve. Of course, animals also have this ability, instinct or gut feeling, which is considered to have been the beginning of our human memory.

Some researchers go so far as to say that important parts of our social abilities may have been developed from – and still be controlled by – bacteria so that they can more easily spread to other individuals. According to this view, we are a kind of vessel that has adapted and been designed according to the microbes' needs to grow and spread.

This would explain why microbes seem to be able to affect both our mood and desires, and thus also our lifestyle choices. Of course this isn't a conscious control but instead an evolutionary result of the microbes' constant struggle for survival.

As we've just said, humans constitute an ecosystem. But in fact we aren't just one ecosystem. Instead, we carry around a number of different ones spread out across areas such as the mouth, nose, armpits, vagina, in the stomach and on the skin and feet. You have different ecosystems on your canine and front teeth. They're even different on the side of a tooth that faces your cheek than they are on the side that faces your tongue. These neighbouring bacterial environments arise early in childhood and then follow you throughout your life.

In many ways, these resident microbes are your most loyal friends. Every time you brush your teeth, billions of them are washed away, but hundreds of thousands remain on each tooth and quickly begin to multiply again. If you don't brush your teeth properly, the bacteria settle more densely in the plaque that your dental hygienist then has to scrape away.

Some of them live in the six-metre-long small intestine, where the majority of food is broken down by our own enzymes. But the majority of them live in the colon, where they attack all of the hard-to-digest left over material that ends up there. Here, different bacteria increase depending on what you give them to eat. And afterwards, 60% of the dry weight you deposit in the toilet consists of microbes. So in purely mathematical terms, there are actually grounds for feeling more human after you've visited the toilet.

In the same way that the environment around us is subject to pressure and change, the fermenting, bubbling world within us is facing challenges on at least as serious a level.

It isn't only tigers and rhinoceroses that are threatened with extinction and risk disappearing from the surface of the planet forever. Deep inside us, the companions that have been with us since the dawn of time are slowly withering and disappearing almost before we even realised they were there – still less what they were for.

While people with a Western, urban lifestyle carry around 600–1,000 different species in their guts, the indigenous peoples in places like the Amazon and Malawi have almost twice as many – often upwards of 1,600 types of gut bacteria. They also have many species that are totally unknown to us. The reason is simple: they eat a much more varied diet than we do, consisting of lots of different fruits, vegetables and herbs.

Because the apparently wide range of choices we're faced with in a normal food shop is largely an illusion. If you look closer at the list of ingredients, you'll constantly encounter the same items, such as wheat, corn, soya, rice, sugar and palm oil. These sorts of foods now dominate in almost the whole Western world. According to a major survey carried out in 2016, three quarters of all food consumed on Earth comes from just 12 plant and five animal species.

When researchers fed mice this type of repetitive, fibre-poor Western food, consisting of a lot of processed fat, meat and fast carbohydrates, the number of species in their gut flora decreased significantly. This reduction in species was then inherited over four mouse generations. In the worst case, every extinct species of gut flora can lead to an ability lost forever. There is a good chance that at some time during the long history of humanity, our gut flora has helped us survive.

Of course some gut bacteria are probably something we can manage without, like when you inherit your grandmother's old christening robe. It's nice to have, but you don't use

it often, and you can cope without it. In other cases, however, we might be losing cornerstones of our immune system, which have always been there for us to rely upon. The lost microbes perhaps had characteristics that protected us against a natural toxin or helped us to break down a component in food.

One example is carbohydrates. While our own genes only help us to manufacture 17 enzymes that break down carbohydrates – and primarily simpler sugars – different gut bacteria can contribute a further almost 16,000 enzymes that break down complex carbohydrates.

Depending on the bacteria we happen to carry ourselves, this means we can have completely different reactions to eating food that contains a lot of carbohydrates. We'll look later at other ways that our gut flora can give us entirely different abilities to tolerate different types of food. In a similar way, these microbes can also determine how your body reacts to medicine your doctor has prescribed.

With this in mind, it isn't surprising that the number of different species that live in the gut is one of the clearest signs of good (or poor) health. The more species that balance each other in a healthy gut flora, the better. Researchers all seem to agree about this.

Pretty much every disease, both physical and mental, has been shown to be associated with a lower number of species in the gut, even if the exact mechanisms regarding cause and effect aren't yet completely understood.

Just like when biological diversity decreases in the Baltic Sea or around a monocropped field, the risk of collapse increases in the gut's own depleted ecosystem. When an individual species is wiped out from a healthy fauna, there's always a similar species that can fill the void. But in an ecosystem that's already disturbed, there's a risk that the balance will be lost. Imbalances can easily arise when individual species get a free hand and can increase explosively.

In this context, the word explosion is something of an understatement. Because if there's one thing bacteria can do, it's multiply. If a single bacterium was able to develop freely with a division every 20 minutes, the total mass after just two days would correspond to that of the entire planet.

That sounds incredible, but work it out for yourself and you'll see. The only thing that prevents this from happening is a shortage of food and constant competition with other microbes. It's this balance of terror that creates stability and helps us to stay healthy.

So what peacekeeping force can we call in to help? You probably won't be surprised if we reveal that the food on your plate plays a completely crucial role. You'll soon understand how they go together.

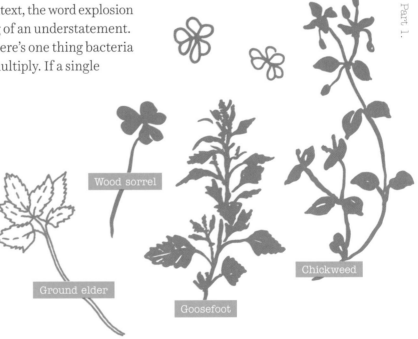

Wood sorrel

Ground elder

Goosefoot

Chickweed

Weed salad with olive oil and hazelnuts

Lots of tasty and healthy herbs have been given the undeserved name of weeds. Like chickweed – probably the most common weed in Sweden – or ground elder – probably the most feared weed. Sweet cicely, which tastes of aniseed, can be tricky to find, although it's common near older gardens. So keep your eyes open next time you go for a walk in the country.

1 bunch of weeds, such as chickweed, sweet cicely, ground elder
2 tablespoons olive oil
½ tablespoon sherry vinegar or red wine vinegar
a pinch of salt
5–6 toasted hazelnuts

1. Pick over and rinse the weeds in cold water.
2. Dry off in a salad spinner or place on a kitchen towel to dry.
3. Mix with olive oil, vinegar and salt.
4. Grate or crush the hazelnuts, and sprinkle over the salad.

Seasonal greens with carrot sauce

Discover spring vegetables! Dare to vary and try out new things. The flavours represent different healthy substances.

300g carrots
100ml water
2 tablespoons chia seeds
3 tablespoons cold-pressed rapeseed oil
1 teaspoon spirit vinegar, 12%
a pinch of salt
2–3 bunches of spring vegetables such as fennel, carrots, asparagus, lettuce, radishes, weeds etc.

1. Peel and grate the carrots. Mix with the water to a smooth consistency.
2. Add the chia seeds and continue to mix until you obtain a cream.
3. Continue to mix and add the oil in an even trickle.
4. Season with the spirit vinegar and salt.
5. Peel or wash the spring vegetables and serve alongside the carrot sauce.

- - - - - - - - - - - - - - - - - - - -

Note! It's important to know what you're doing when picking edible plants in the wild!

- - - - - - - - - - - - - - - - - - - -

Left: Weed salad with olive oil and hazelnuts. Right: Seasonal greens with carrot sauce. (See page 25)

Raw butternut squash and ginger soup

We've got a bit tired of all these 'shots'. Why not use the same ingredients to make tasty food that stimulates both your taste buds and immune system simultaneously? Here's a delicious soup full of healthy fibre, anti-inflammatory ginger and immune-strengthening turmeric.

500g butternut squash
2 cloves of garlic
3cm fresh ginger
2cm fresh turmeric (or 1 teaspoon
    dried ground)
300ml water
1 teaspoon ground caraway
1 teaspoon ground coriander seeds
1 tablespoon lemon juice
2 tablespoons virgin coconut oil
1 teaspoon salt
100g cashew nuts

1. Peel the butternut squash, garlic, ginger and turmeric. Grate coarsely and place in a saucepan.
2. Add the water and heat to 40°C.
3. Cover with clingfilm and leave to stand for 30 minutes.
4. Pour into a blender and mix until smooth.
5. Add the dry spices, lemon juice, coconut oil and salt and continue to mix for 1 minute.
6. Add the cashew nuts and mix until you obtain a smooth, creamy consistency. Add more nuts if required.
7. Season with more salt, lemon juice and spices to taste.

Note! You need a strong blender!

PRESENTING:

YOUR GUT

FLORA

CHAPTER 2.

News update!

We're in the middle of the biological revolution. Within the space of just a few decades, our view of ourselves and our health – and probably our ageing too – will have fundamentally changed. And our knowledge of gut bacteria is part of this.

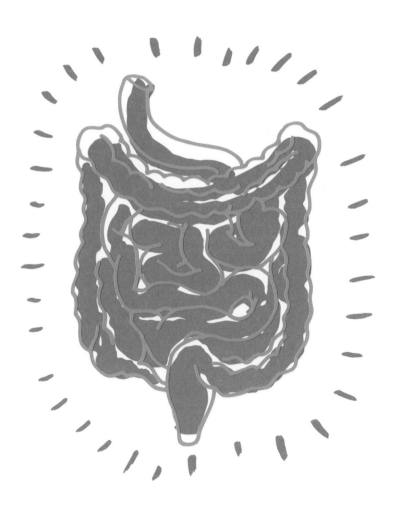

One new insight is that, like farmers, we can look after and cultivate our gut flora with all its varying bacteria, viruses, archaea, yeasts, phages and sometimes even parasites and other organisms.

At about the age of three, our gut flora, with its hundreds of different species, achieves an equilibrium that's so unique for each individual that it can be compared to an individual fingerprint. And yet all of our gut flora try to carry out largely the same biological functions. But that gets more difficult the more bacteria we lose.

Despite the fact that we all have an individual gut flora that finds a completely individual balance, there's still a core of about 40 different types of bacteria that often recur and constitute a kind of frame for the human species.

If we could put on special spectacles that allowed us to see all the microbes around us, we'd quickly see that this type of mutually stable ecosystem covers essentially every surface on earth. One example is when you're paddling at the water's edge in the summer, and you put your foot on a stone covered with slippery algae. The entire stone has a thin covering consisting of microbes, not unlike what we have in the gut.

Every pinch of soil contains billions of bacteria. A few live several kilometres down in the bedrock, others float around in the air, some microbes can survive in space and were perhaps what first brought life to our planet – and some bored researcher once calculated that the quantity of viruses in the planet's seas alone correspond to the mass of 175,000 blue whales.

Even our skin and insides are coated with a protective microbial film. And this is completely different at different points. In your armpits and on your forehead, you have lots of bacteria but relatively few species. Meanwhile, on your hands you have fewer bacteria but lots of different species.

The bacterial flora on your right and left hand are so different – but still stable – that it would be easy to measure which fingers I use to press different keys on my laptop by taking samples from the keys.

We wander through a private cloud where we release approximately 35 million bacteria an hour, mainly from our skin and mouths. So it's no wonder that bacterial traces have already been used in the TV series *CSI: Miami*.

And yes, there are differences in the microbes on the skin that explain why some of us get more acne as teenagers and why some of us are more prone to mosquito bites than others. Different skin bacteria attract different sorts of mosquitoes to different body parts. For example, the most common malaria mosquito is primarily attracted to the hands.

The biggest benefit of the skin bacteria is probably that they occupy space and prevent yeasts and other aggressive microbes from dominating. It's common for the skin's bacterial flora to change or decrease in cases of eczema or the skin disease psoriasis. New research also indicates that some skin bacteria have a protective effect against skin cancer.

In 2018, Chinese researchers reported that people living in big cities have a reduced and less varied set of skin bacteria than those living in the countryside or in small towns. They suggested that this could be one cause of increased problems with eczema and skin diseases.

- -

Sweat is good for your skin

Sweat is thought to contribute to good health because it provides food to a natural and healthy set of skin bacteria.

Our sweat contains quite a lot of ammonia and nitrates, and therefore attracts a particular type of bacteria that lives on these substances. They transform sweat into nitrites and nitric oxide, which is rapidly absorbed by the skin. These substances help us to regulate both blood pressure and the immune system. The problem is that these skin bacteria are very sensitive to antibacterial agents such as triclosan, and have therefore been largely wiped out in high income countries.

Source: WHO report on biological diversity (2015)

- -

Courgette salad with mint and lemon

A fresh side dish with a wonderful balance of mint and lemon. Just like many other herbs, mint is full of vitamins, minerals and other healthy substances. Many cultures use relatively large quantities of herbs, so don't skimp on the amounts.

1 courgette
1 teaspoon salt
1 lemon
2 tablespoons olive oil
4–8 mint leaves or edible flowers

1. Slice the courgette thinly lengthways with a mandoline or sharp knife.
2. Mix with the salt and leave to stand at room temperature for 30 minutes.
3. Squeeze the liquid out of the courgette.
4. Zest the lemon and set to one side.
5. Squeeze the lemon juice and mix with the courgette and olive oil.
6. Top with torn mint leaves or edible flowers in season, and scatter over the lemon zest.

Salmon tartare with horseradish and mustard

Salmon tartare is a tasty, festive starter that's quick to prepare. And of course salmon is full of healthy Omega-3 fatty acids. Horseradish gets a little less attention, but it doesn't merely give a fresh flavour – it's also a really good source of both fibre and various minerals.

400g salmon, boneless
   and skinless
2 egg yolks
2 tablespoons chopped shallots
1 tablespoon spirit vinegar, 12%
2 tablespoons coarse grain
   mustard
small pinch of salt
1 bunch of mixed leaves and
   weeds (e.g. spinach, chard,
   dandelion leaves, rocket)
8–12 tomatoes (seasonal –
   preferably yellow cocktail)
small pinch of black pepper,
   freshly ground
1 horseradish root, approx. 5cm,
   peeled and grated
3 tablespoons cold-pressed
   rapeseed oil

1. Cut the salmon into approx. 1–2cm cubes.
2. Mix the salmon, egg yolks, chopped shallots, spirit vinegar, mustard and salt. Leave to marinate for 10 minutes.
3. Pick over and rinse the green leaves. Tear into small pieces or shred.
4. Cut the tomatoes into 2–3cm cubes.
5. Place the salmon tartare on plates, season with a pinch of black pepper and top with the tomatoes, green leaves and grated horseradish. Drizzle over a little rapeseed oil.

Happy Food snack platter

Create a plate that explodes with colour! You'll be happy just looking at it! Colours helped our ancestors to find berries and fruit to eat, and it's no coincidence that the healthiest ingredients are the most colourful. It's the colour itself that's the healthy bit.

fresh fruit and vegetables
raw honey
nuts
sea salt flakes
crackers, optional

1. Wash and cut the fruit and vegetables into bite-sized pieces.
2. Serve on a large platter with raw honey, nuts, salt and crackers, if desired.

- - - - - - - - - - - - - - - - - - - -

Note! Use seasonal berries, fruit, vegetables, leaves, seeds and nuts.

- - - - - - - - - - - - - - - - - - - -

ONE WITH NATURE

CHAPTER 3.

Shinrin-yoku
– forest bathing

Epidemics of obesity, diabetes, food allergies, bowel diseases, depression and a long list of other illnesses can no longer be seen as isolated phenomena that can be cured by means of medication or individual probiotic bacteria. The problem is much bigger than that. So says well-known allergy researcher Susan Prescott. According to Prescott, we must quite simply begin to see all of these diseases as parts of a whole that are propelled by the same forces.

Susan Prescott has participated in a number of the allergy studies that in recent years have made authorities re-evaluate their recommendations – for example, no longer advising against giving healthy children peanuts.

Prescott says that our own bacterial flora is an inseparable part of the world of microbes that has populated the Earth for three billion years, while humans only developed during the last three million years. The depletion of and imbalances in our gut flora reflect disruptions that we have ourselves caused in our environment.

Without understanding the whole, we can never halt diseases, according to Prescott.

At a scientific conference I attended in 2017, Susan Prescott expanded upon her reasoning.

'Life on Earth is under great pressure. We're in the middle of climate change, environmental destruction and a huge reduction in biological diversity. Many diseases are developing in parallel with urbanisation and the expansion of the modern Western lifestyle. This pattern includes a movement away from traditional food cultures and close contact with nature that all of

our ancestors experienced right up
to the modern day.'

The roots of humanity can
be found in nature, and
ultimately we are constantly
and unconsciously pulled in
that direction to feel good.

'From the beginning, we
were in balance with nature – in
symbiosis. What we're seeing now
is a movement towards imbalance,
dysbiosis,' she explained.

In one eloquent experiment,
South Korean researchers exposed
people to alternating images of
nature and urban environments.
The nature images were perfectly
ordinary, not magnificent sunsets
over the Himalayas, for example.

It turned out that the nature
images consistently activated parts
of the brain that are associated
with positive feelings, emotional
stability, the desire to share,
empathy and love.

The images of urban
environments instead activated
– in an equally unambiguous way –
the amygdala, the walnut-sized part
of the brain that handles fear and
reacts to threats. Overstimulation
of the amygdala is usually linked
to an increased risk of things like
panic attacks.

But the benefits don't stop
at us feeling better if we have
nature before our eyes. Taking
as a starting point what in Japan
is called shinrin-yoku – in other
words, bathing in the forest and
forest air while walking – Japanese
researchers have discovered that
forest walks can lower blood sugar
in diabetes patients.

The first organised research into
shinrin-yoku began in the 1990s on
the island of Yakushima, which is
known for its biological diversity –
and for being the inspiration for the
film *Princess Mononoke* by Hayao
Miyazaki. Nearly 30 years later, it's
clear that walking doesn't merely
give you fresh air. Separate studies
have shown how our nervous
system and our ability to handle
stress are positively affected when
we see nature, listen to natural
sounds, touch soil, stones or plants
and are bathed in the invisible
chemicals given off by trees.

When we inhale, we breathe
nature into our lungs. Every
cubic centimetre of air contains
enormous quantities of
small particles. For example,
gammaproteobacteria float
in the air above both soil and
plants, and these are considered
to be particularly important
in counteracting eczema and
promoting healthy skin.

Urban environments are often
dominated by various sorts of air
pollution, while in the natural

environment we are surrounded by microscopic fragments of leaves, seeds, pollen, dead insects and the bacteria living on all of these. Ongoing research indicates that the microbes floating in the air don't merely stick to our skin, but can also enter our bodies through both the skin and our mouths and noses, where they can affect our gut flora.

In other words, by being surrounded by nature, you're bathing in biological diversity.

The conclusion that can be drawn from the research is that as an organism, humans perceive, embrace and understand nature as an old friend.

According to this research, in our modern society, we sometimes try to silence our inherited longing for nature with consumption. Because what is the appeal of glittering jewellery if not a millennia-long inherited attraction to the rays of the sun reflected from fresh, running water?

Shinrin-yoku has inspired researchers all round the world, who have reported that access to green areas positively affects human mental health. The effect also seems to be stronger the more types of plants are grown in the area. But that's not all – the more types of plants you see through your window, the less you produce of the stress hormone cortisol.

In the UK, the number of bird species have been shown to be an excellent marker of health among people living in the area. And in Finland, researcher Tari Haahtela at Helsinki University has reported that allergies and asthma are uncommon in environments where there are lots of butterflies. Insects are a sign of a healthy ecosystem with great biological diversity.

And biological diversity is all about how viable our planet is. An environment that's burgeoning with life helps us feel healthy and alive – it benefits our immune system and our recovery ability and creates a kind of elastic bandage, explains allergy researcher Susan Prescott.

'Because all life on earth is interwoven, a continued reduction in biological diversity cannot be without consequences for human health.'

On the small scale, we can try to create meals characterised by great variety and biological diversity.

The evidence is piling up. Reduced diversity is taking its toll, Prescott concludes.

Whole grilled sea bass
with green vegetables

At the beginning of time, our ancestors wandered along
the African coastline. Perhaps it was eating fish and shellfish
full of Omega-3 fatty acids that made their brains grow. In
any case, that's one theory. More intelligent or not, is there
anything more tasty than freshly caught fish?

1–2 whole sea bass (or you could
use mackerel, perch or zander)
8–12 mint leaves
3 cloves of garlic
8–12 coriander leaves
2 green chillies
3 tablespoons olive oil
1 tablespoon lime juice
2 tablespoons soy sauce
1 bunch of haricots verts
4 heads of pak choi
coriander leaves, mint leaves,
green chilli and lime wedges
for serving
sea salt

1. Preheat the grill to high, or light
the barbeque.
2. Scale, gut and remove the gills
from the fish.
3. Salt the fish thoroughly. Tie the
fish with kitchen twine or place
in a barbecue basket.
4. Grill for 6–8 minutes on each
side so that the fish is nicely
browned.
5. Blend the mint, garlic,
coriander, chilli, olive oil, lime
juice and soy sauce into a
dressing.
6. Pick over the beans and pak
choi. Blanch in salted water for
30 seconds.
7. Serve immediately with the
freshly-grilled sea bass and
herb dressing.
8. Top with fresh coriander and
mint leaves, sliced green chilli
and lime wedges.

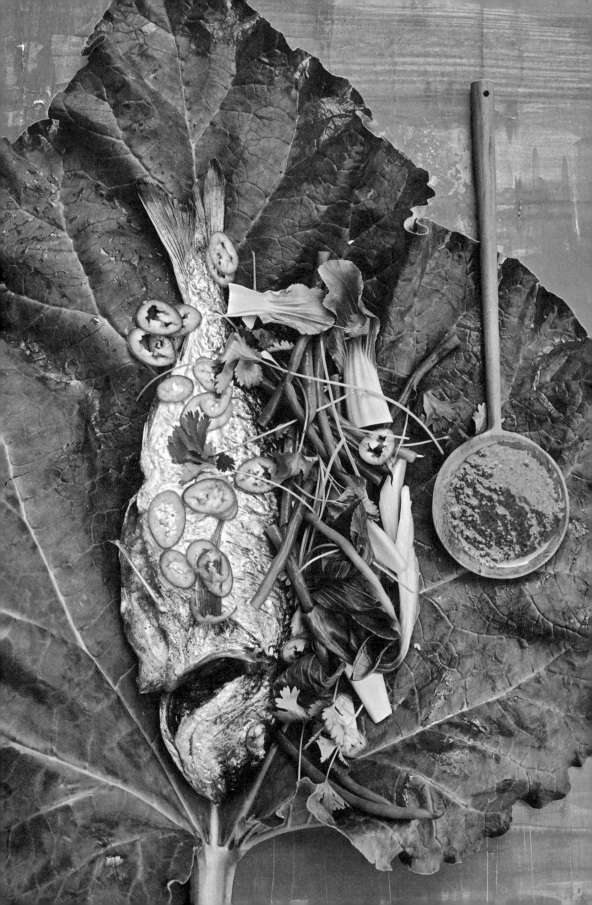

Roasted carrots with rocket, goat's cheese, pumpkin seeds and orange

So easy, so beautiful and so tasty. But don't harmful substances form if you heat carrots to such a high temperature? Our answer: ingredients full of antioxidants give protection, but don't let them burn. They're at their best when they have just started to brown.

2 bunches of carrots
3 tablespoons olive oil
6–8 sprigs of thyme
3 tablespoons pumpkin seeds
1 orange
100g goat's cheese
1 bunch of rocket
salt

1. Peel the carrots and cut them lengthways.
2. Preheat the oven to 200°C. Place the carrots on a baking sheet with 1 tablespoon of the olive oil, the sprigs of thyme and a pinch of salt.
3. Bake in the oven until the carrots are nicely browned – about 25 minutes.
4. Toast the pumpkin seeds in a dry frying pan over a medium heat.
5. Grate the orange peel and squeeze the juice. Mix with the remaining olive oil and a pinch of salt.
6. Top the carrots with goat's cheese, orange dressing, rocket and toasted pumpkin seeds.

Note! Leave the oven door open a little to release the moisture when the carrots are roasting!

DIZZYING

NEW RESEARCH

CHAPTER 4.

Researcher: 'We'll forever change how we look at food'

Mapping the human gut flora is progressing at breathtaking speed. Biologist Rob Knight is one of the researchers leading the charge. He's been involved in founding the American Gut Project, with more than 10,000 people already having sent in samples of their own bacteria.

Rob Knight is a 40-year-old New Zealander and former child prodigy. He gained a PhD in ecology and evolutionary biology from Princeton at the age of just 24. Initially, he studied invasive animal species, which are a major problem in his home country, but he soon began to take an interest in invaders among the significantly smaller organisms we carry inside us.

In parallel, he cultivated a talent for handling digital data and developed advanced IT models to analyse the genome of microbes. Soon researchers from all over the world turned to Rob Knight for help, and this is one of the reasons why his name constantly recurs among the authors of the most important scientific articles published on the subject in the last ten years.

Now Rob Knight is a professor at the University of California, San Diego, where he runs his own laboratory. I met him at a scientific conference in Austin, Texas, in spring 2018, where he was one of the key speakers. We had a long conversation about the current state of research and the threats and opportunities he sees in the future.

And we quickly got onto the subject of how artificial intelligence can help us understand connections. For Rob Knight, the development of modern biological research is impossible without advanced computer technology – an opinion he is not alone in holding.

Earlier the same day, he had taken part in a panel debate with Jo Handelsman, who was scientific adviser to Barack Obama.

Jo Handelsman explained that 'just a few years ago, we thought the human genome was extremely complex. Now we're faced with something that's hundreds or thousands of times more complicated.'

Rob: There are more bacteria in your gut than there are stars in the Milky Way. And the gut flora varies from person to person. While you and I share 99.99% of our genes, we share perhaps 10% of our bacteria. This can explain variations between us when it comes to weight, allergies and why some people become sick or anxious more easily than others. When you study how the gut flora affect health, you quickly find yourself faced with more data than any human can handle. This makes the gut flora the ultimate source of what's usually called Big Data and which is ideal for analysis by computers with artificial intelligence – AI.

Henrik: Do you think that in the future bacteria will replace normal medicine? Will it be bugs instead of drugs?

Rob: I think it will be both bugs and drugs – both bacteria and normal medicine – but also that we'll learn to use viruses, metabolites and what are known as phages. Viruses

and bacteria have fought a war for billions of years. They've developed their own arsenals of weapons and protection that we can use, and we're already testing viruses to wipe out some cancer cells. I believe that quite soon we'll be able to cure and prevent many diseases by adding bacteria and other microbes to fill holes in the immune system. And then there are many diseases, such as Crohn's disease and obesity, that can be prevented just using normal good food.

Henrik: So common diseases may be associated with imbalances in the gut flora?

Rob: In recent decades, infectious diseases have decreased, while obesity, diabetes, bowel diseases and other immunological diseases have increased significantly. The link between imbalances in the gut flora and many of the diseases that are increasing is already clear, even if we need more studies to investigate mechanisms and causal relationships. New findings are being made all the time, such as the fact that transplants into mice of faecal material from patients with Parkinson's produce Parkinson's symptoms in the mice. These are new results, but it's still basic research and there's a long way to go until we're treating people.

Henrik: How can obesity be affected by the gut flora?

Rob: We know that people with obesity have more of certain bacteria and we can transfer a predisposition for obesity from humans to mice by transplanting faecal matter. Bacteria can affect how many calories the body absorbs from food. But bacteria also affect eating behaviour. If we have a mouse with sterile gut flora and give it a particular kind of bacteria, it gets fat (the bacteria affect the mouse's feelings of hunger). The only way to prevent the mouse from getting fat is to keep it in a cage without much food – but then it goes mad with hunger. But there is actually another way, and that's to kill the bacteria that cause the feelings of hunger with antibiotics.

Henrik: How did other researchers react to these discoveries?

Rob: When we discovered this, everyone thought it was completely crazy and that this couldn't be the cause. So several other groups investigated it too. In people, it's probably not just one bacteria, but several interacting that cause this.

Henrik: So you mean that the spread of obesity can literally be an infectious epidemic?

Rob: I'm worried that the epidemic of obesity that's spreading across the world can be linked with the spread of bacteria that cause obesity. This type of bacteria thrives when we eat junk food that contains a lot of poor fats and sugar. Obesity and its bacteria often occur in groups. If one person in a family is fat, the others often are too – and they have the same bacteria. If the family have a dog, even the dog is usually overweight.

Henrik: How strong is the evidence that the gut flora is connected to the brain?

Rob: Very strong. Five years ago, the discussion was about whether there was this type of communication at all. Today we know that there are a number of different contact paths in both directions, and so the discussion is more about which of these is most important. This is the very hottest research area just now; the one that everyone wants to be involved in.

Henrik: You've done field studies with a number of indigenous people – the Hadza in Africa and the Yanomami in the Amazon, who were first discovered in 2008. What did they teach you?

Rob: It appears that there's been a

depletion of our gut flora. They have such a completely different lifestyle, which involves them eating a really varied diet and they have a totally different and what appears to be a much healthier and more versatile gut flora. They have a hard life and they have more parasites and infections, but no Crohn's disease or MS. I studied the Hadza in east Africa in 2014, and none of them have Type 2 diabetes. Western diseases are now spreading across the entire world, but you don't see them at all in indigenous peoples or other groups that have been studied in places like Papua New Guinea.

Henrik: You've expressed concern that overconsumption of antibiotics can contribute to an increase in food allergies and other autoimmune diseases.

Rob: I think it's good to think of your gut flora as if it was a garden. If you spray pesticides that wipe out everything, you'll end up with a low variation in the plants that grow there, and what comes back first and takes over are weeds. And the same thing happens in the human digestive system.

Antibiotics, together with vaccines, are the greatest victories in medical history and have saved uncountable numbers of lives. Without antibiotics, countless women would die during childbirth, a bad tooth would suddenly become potentially fatal ... practically all surgery requires antibiotics and the same is true of medical care for premature children – there are many fields in healthcare based on the fact that we have antibiotics.

But there's a downside. The bacteria you carry inside you are a central component in your immune system. When you take a course of antibiotics, the first infection is often cured but then it takes up to three months before your immune system recovers and during that time you're particularly sensitive to new attacks. Some of the protective bacterial species you carry may be wiped out completely. And perhaps they were exactly the bacteria that specialised in breaking down some component in food that you can't tolerate afterwards.

Henrik: Can this be contributing to the significant increase in food allergies?

Rob: Yes, the gut flora and immune system are at their most sensitive in small children who are still developing. We see a strong connection between imbalances in the gut flora and gluten intolerance, although there are still question marks around cause and effect, and there's also support for a link between asthma and food allergies. The same can also apply to other immunological diseases that are now greatly increasing. It's well established that lifestyle and environment are important. If you live on a farm with animals, it's unlikely that you'll develop allergies.

I believe that in the future we'll be just as horrified over today's unthinking use of antibiotics as we are about the fact that people used to drink radioactive water and paint their houses with radioactive paint. Today this seems like a terrible idea, but it was once considered to be fun in one case and healthy in the other – and after all, what could go wrong?

Henrik: So what should you eat to develop a healthy gut flora?

Rob: Well, for example, if you eat huge quantities of your favourite vegetable, such as broccoli or Brussels sprouts, that's probably not a great idea. The best thing to do is instead to eat a wide variety of plants, ideally of different colours that give you different sorts of nutrients and bioactive substances. Different bioactive substances affect your gut flora in ways that we're only just beginning to understand. Eating lots of different plants also seems to have a much greater importance than whether or not you eat meat.

Don't eat so much sugar or so much finely ground white flour, because that nourishes harmful bacteria. But you should eat a lot of fibre that reaches the colon and provides food for your gut bacteria, together with different coloured vegetables.

Henrik: Is resistant starch good? (Found, for example, in beans, potatoes and green bananas.)

Rob: When it comes to resistant starch, there's solid data that indicates an effect on obesity and diabetes. We're also trying to find out whether it's anti-inflammatory. The disadvantage is if you take it to extremes and only eat resistant starch – then it's likely to produce side-effects. So the important lesson is to eat a varied diet and not just one thing.

Henrik: Fermented foods?

Rob: People have been eating food like sauerkraut and yoghurt for centuries. I encourage my children to eat fermented foods and I eat them myself. Personally I like Icelandic skyr, but that's mainly because it tastes good. You have to be conscious of the fact that so far there is very little evidence that fermented foods give either you or your children any great health gains except to a very limited extent. We need more research. Another problem is that many types of yoghurt contain added sugar that instead upset the gut flora.

Ten years ago when we started mapping the human gut flora, there wasn't much money in probiotic bacteria. Today, largely due to the basic research we and other researchers have carried out, probiotics have become a billion-dollar industry that so far is completely unregulated. Many health claims are made that quite simply lack any scientific basis. Our own random samples of products have also shown that they often don't actually contain the bacteria stated on the label.

Henrik: Are there any other ways to boost your gut flora?

Rob: Yes, new findings that have surprised us are the major advantages of good sleep and short-term fasting. I'm not talking about fasting for entire days, but instead limiting eating to eight hours in the day. When we compared the effect of eating vegan food for three months with this kind of short-term fasting, the positive effects were greater from short-term fasting.

Henrik: In your latest book, *Dirt is Good*, you and your colleague Jack

Gilbert recommend that parents allow their children to eat soil. Is that a good idea?

Rob: We think so, even if more research is required. In many traditional cultures, it's been considered healthy to eat clay, and animals often do this too. There are very few harmful bacteria in normal soil. But our point isn't that you should eat soil on a regular basis, but instead that it's not dangerous if small children are playing outdoors and happen to eat some soil. You don't have to immediately scrub dirty fingers with soap and water. Thumb suckers and nail biters actually get fewer allergies. We've changed our lifestyle in such a way that small children are no longer confronted with foreign bacteria to the same extent, and that means their immune systems don't develop as well.

Henrik: So what's the most important thing you see happening in the future?

Rob: There'll be significantly more personal advice. And the technology will continue to change a great deal. When you can take your smartphone and scan your own faeces for imbalances that can damage your health, and then go out to the shop or restaurant and scan the food to fill the voids, it will completely change everything for anyone working with food.

In the future, we'll have smart toilets that analyse your faeces in real time and smart bathroom mirrors that sense the imbalances in your mouth and on your breath. Our goal is to achieve a microbial compass that helps us to optimise diet, exercise, medicines, sleep and all the other things that affect your bacterial flora. We already have all the components. We simply have to put them together in a new and user-friendly way.

Rob's 5 pieces of advice

Eat a varied diet: It's more about how many different sorts of plants you eat than how much of them you eat. Eat multi-coloured food.

Eat soil: Allow your children to play and get dirty with soil. Soil is a microbial paradise with more than a billion bacteria in every gram, but few of them can make your child sick. Of course you should use common sense and watch out for obvious contamination. In animal tests, several soil bacteria have been shown to have an anti-inflammatory effect, reduce anxiety symptoms and counteract asthma.

Get a dog: According to one study, children who grow up with a dog have a 13% lower risk of being

affected by asthma than other children. For children who grow up on a farm, the risk is halved. A 2018 Dutch study showed that those growing up within 500 metres of a pig farm or 400 metres of a farm with cows were less allergic than those who had grown up just a few hundred metres further away. Every extra farm in the neighbourhood reduced the risk of allergies by 4%.

Wash your dishes by hand: In families where the dishes are washed by hand, more bacteria survive and there is on average less asthma and allergies than in families which always use a dishwasher. In the same way, it's sufficient to wipe off the draining board and worktop with normal soap rather than with strong bactericidal agents. Moderation is best when it comes to cleaning.

Air your home: Open your windows and air your home as often as possible. The dust that leaves through the windows contains microscopic skin flakes and weathered building materials, and in float minute particles from plants with bacteria that enhance your own flora and fine-tune your immune system.

Spiced aubergine

A variant of the aubergine dip baba ganoush is an essential on any mezze platter, and is also the perfect complement to a range of different dishes. Here the chilli gives a little extra bite.

1 aubergine
2 shallots
3 cloves of garlic
1 red chilli
4 tablespoons olive oil
2 teaspoons caraway seeds
1 lemon
2 tablespoons tahini
1 teaspoon salt
100g parsley
edible flowers

1. Cut the aubergine into 2cm cubes.
2. Fry without oil in a large frying pan over a medium-high heat for 6–8 minutes.
3. Peel and slice the shallots and garlic. Slice the chilli. Place the shallots, garlic and chilli in a saucepan.
4. Add the olive oil and caraway seeds and fry over a low heat until the shallots and garlic are soft.
5. Mix with the aubergine and leave to cool.
6. Grate the lemon zest and squeeze the lemon juice.
7. Season the aubergine mixture with the lemon zest and juice, tahini, salt and parsley.
8. Serve at room temperature, topped with edible flowers, with toasted sourdough bread or as an accompaniment to grilled fish.

Gnocchi with sunflower seed pesto

Garlic, olive oil, basil, Parmesan. This dish is like a warm Mediterranean wind blowing across your palate. And if you're doubtful about carbohydrates, why not eat a smaller portion?

3 tablespoons sunflower seeds
2 cloves of garlic
100g basil leaves
a pinch of salt
2 tablespoons olive oil
500g gnocchi
100g Parmesan

1. Toast the sunflower seeds until golden brown in a dry frying pan over a medium-high heat for 3–4 minutes.
2. Peel the garlic and coarsely chop the basil. Place in a mortar and add the salt.
3. Grind the garlic and basil, then add a little oil at a time.
4. Add the sunflower seeds and grind together until you obtain a creamy consistency. Add more olive oil if it's too dry.
5. Cook the gnocchi in lightly salted water until it is al dente. Drain off the water and leave to steam.
6. Stir the pesto into the gnocchi and serve with Parmesan shavings.

Tomato salad with homemade cream cheese

It's easy to make your own cream cheese. It does take a little while, but much of that is resting time, so you can actually spend a lot of the time doing something else.

2–8 tomatoes, mixed colours
1 shallot
2 tablespoons olive oil
small pinch of salt
2–8 fresh oregano leaves

Cream cheese
1 litre milk
200ml cream
4 tablespoons lemon juice
small pinch of salt

1. Heat the milk and cream to 34°C.
2. Remove from the heat. Add the lemon juice and stir carefully until it separates. Set to one side for 30 minutes.
3. Stir the milk to see if it has coagulated (if not, bring the milk to a simmer again and repeat step 2).
4. Pour through a coffee filter or cheesecloth and allow the whey to run off.
5. Suspend in the filter or cheesecloth until a creamy 'cream cheese' remains. This takes about an hour (the longer it's suspended, the drier the cheese).
6. Season with salt.
7. Halve the tomatoes and peel and slice the shallot. Mix with the olive oil and salt.
8. Top with the cream cheese and fresh oregano to serve.

WHAT MOST AFFECTS YOUR GUT FLORA?

CHAPTER 5.

The researchers' top list

Researchers for the American Gut Project have compiled a range of test results to compare the factors that most contribute to a healthy gut flora. Here is their top list.

1. Eat a varied range of plants. We get by far the biggest effect on our gut flora by eating more varied vegetables and fruit – from less than five different types per week to more than 30. But even increasing from five to ten different types a week gives major benefits, according to researchers. Alternate between different types of lettuce, cabbage plants, whole grains, legumes, alliums, fruit and berries. Make sure you get as many different types of fibre, colours and flavours as possible on your plate.

2. Age. Your gut flora says a lot about your age. We're born with a largely sterile gut flora, and the foundations are laid in the first three years of life. By about the age of 20, the gut flora is fully established. The variation then begins to diminish, and as we age we develop an increasingly large proportion of toxic pro-inflammatory bacteria. When

we age, it's important to continue to eat fibre-rich food.

3. IBD. If you have an inflammatory bowel disease (IBD), your gut flora is strongly out of balance, fluctuates significantly and sometimes more resembles the bacterial flora on the skin or in the mouth.

4. The season. The season affects how much fresh fruit and vegetables we eat, and sunlight contributes vitamin D which positively affects our microbes. But it's probably just as important that when it's warmer we get outdoors and take more exercise, breathe in fresh air and take in more of the enormous diversity of bacteria found in the natural environment.

5. Antibiotics. Don't hesitate to use antibiotics to get rid of dangerous infections. But the gains don't come for free, because antibiotics sweep everything before them. It

63

can take three months or more before your gut flora and immune system recover, and on the way you may have lost some important companions forever.

6. Gender. Adult men and women have differences in their gut flora, but it's too early to say why and what that means. One hypothesis is that our sex hormones play a role, and another is that differences could explain why women are more often affected by auto-immune diseases. During pregnancy and breastfeeding, dramatic changes can take place in women's gut flora, which are intended for the foetus. A well known side effect of these changes is that pregnant women get cravings for certain sorts of food, more easily gain weight, can become nauseous, and in the worst case are affected by diabetes and depression.

7. Sleep. A normal night's sleep of around seven hours and at fixed times seems to be the optimal way of achieving a healthy gut flora. A lack of sleep, but also too much sleep, seems to have the opposite effect. The bacteria have their own daily rhythm, and sleep problems are closely associated with disrupted gut flora.

8. Obesity. There's a clear connection between BMI (body mass index) and the gut flora. People with obesity often have a higher proportion of pro-inflammatory gut bacteria. This type of bacteria can then reduce as they lose weight. Some bacteria can make the body's energy uptake from food increase by up to 15%. So in other words, some people gain weight more easily than others. The bacteria can also affect feelings of hunger and satiety.

9. Alcohol. One or two glasses of wine a day do no harm (if you can stick to that level), but more than this is negative for the gut flora.

10. Exercise. It's very good for both body and brain to exercise, but the effect on the gut flora isn't always positive, particularly if you're not in good shape, have poor eating habits or an unbalanced gut from the beginning, or in the case of extreme endurance training. All exercise produces pro-inflammatory stress for the body, which means it is particularly important to eat well to avoid exercise leading to symptoms of illness.

Medications

In 2018, German researchers warned that they had examined 923 normal medicines which were not antibiotic and discovered that 250 of them killed or in some other way affected at least one of the 40 bacterial species that are most common in a healthy gut flora.

The effect on these core bacteria was described as frightening, given that many of the medicines are the kind of things that people take for a long time, such as antidepressants and stomach ulcer medicines. 'In all probability, the effect is actually still greater. We measured only 40 of the roughly 1,000 common bacteria that occur in the gut,' says Peer Bork, Head of Research at the European Molecular Biology Laboratory (EMBL). He adds that the doses used correspond to those given during normal treatment.

Peer Bork emphasises that it is currently impossible to say in each individual case whether the effects on the gut bacteria will be positive or negative. Sometimes it is the toxin-producing bacteria which are wiped out, and sometimes those belonging to a healthy flora. These effects are sometimes a previously unknown aspect of the medication's health-giving impact. At other times, they can be because of side-effects or because the medication is less effective for some people.

'This is the first time it has been investigated, and I'm convinced that this is really important. In the future, doctors prescribing longer treatments will have to take into account how the medication affects the individual patient's gut flora,' says Peer Bork.

Another discovery that researchers at the EMBL made was that many of the medicines also led to antibiotic resistance. Bork said, 'That was a surprise. Antibiotic resistance is a major problem and our findings now show that we must be careful not only when prescribing antibiotics. Even completely different medications can lead to antibiotic resistance'.

Salt

For thousands of years, salt has been used as a preservative which prevents bacteria from multiplying. So it isn't so surprising that salty food affects the gut flora. Our bodies need salt, but not a great deal, and the World Health Organisation (WHO) has for many years warned that today's food is too salty and contributes to high blood pressure.

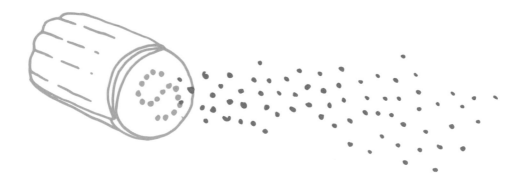

Surprisingly, however, it is only recently that researchers have begun to investigate how salt affects the gut bacteria. And the results weren't long in arriving.

In November 2017, researchers reported that salt reduces the quantity of healthy lactic acid bacteria that help us to feel well, and also triggers pro-inflammatory immune cells, which in turn lead to conditions including increased blood pressure. The clear inhibitory effect of salt on lactic acid bacteria can explain why people in the Western world have significantly fewer beneficial bacteria than traditional indigenous populations. As a child, we have large numbers of these, but they disappear when we grow up, probably as a consequence of too much salt.

Fasting

People in different cultures throughout the ages have fasted – and this is hardly a coincidence. Today we know that calorie restriction is the most effective method thus far of making test animals live longer. But this involves, for example, mice who, for their entire lives, are served food which is low-calorie but extremely nutrient dense, to avoid vitamin and mineral deficiencies. The increased lifetime of the mice would equate to around 150 years for humans.

The explanation seems to be that the body's cells have two basic settings. One is for good times when there is a lot of food. In this case, the cells grow, live, multiply and then age and die. All at breakneck speed.

The other setting involves coping with periods of famine. At these times, the body's cells go into a kind of survival mode where it's more important to hang on to what you have until food is available again. In other words, a kind of feast and famine on cellular level. As modern humans, we live in a surplus society, where in theory we're in a constant feast mode, with the pedal to the floor right to the end.

Unfortunately, lifetime calorie restriction is not a fun diet, or, as one researcher I interviewed expressed it slightly ironically: 'In any case, it would make your life feel longer.'

Instead, various types of fake fasting diets have been developed which it's a little easier to put up with. One is the extremely low carbohydrate ketogenic diet, which was initially developed to treat people with epilepsy. Fasting was excellent for them, but as soon as they began to eat again their attacks returned. For many people who are subject to severe epilepsy, a ketogenic diet turned out to function very well, and this also applies to many people with a blood sugar imbalance.

Different types of short-term fasting or fasting every other day is another way of trying to reap the attractive benefits of lifetime calorie restrictions without having to put up with its privations.

Because fasting every other day is difficult, the 5:2 diet was created. This involves eating 500 calories a day for two days a week, and eating normally for the rest of the time. This is not likely to markedly extend your life, but in any case it seems to make those who do it feel better.

So how good is short-term fasting for the gut flora? Well, in fact it's excellent. In one trial where overweight people were put on a fasting diet for six weeks, their gut flora improved radically. But the best form of fasting for the gut seems to be the variant that's normally called 16:8. This means eating as much as possible of the day's food during eight waking hours and allowing your stomach to rest for the remainder of the time.

An Israeli study recently showed that diabetics were healthiest when they ate a substantial breakfast, a medium-size lunch, a small dinner and no snacks at all. A slice of bread consumed in the morning produced a lower increase in insulin and less fat storage than exactly the same slice of bread consumed in the evening.

If you consider this more carefully, you realise that this is how people have eaten in the majority of older cultures where the daily rhythm is governed by the sun. They have often got up early in the morning and only eaten something very light then had a substantial breakfast some way into the morning. Then they have come home for dinner as early as four o'clock and gone to bed quite early.

These patterns may have varied somewhat, but without doubt none of our ancestors have forced their stomachs to work as much and as persistently as modern humans. And the daily rhythm is incredibly important – which leads us to the importance of rest.

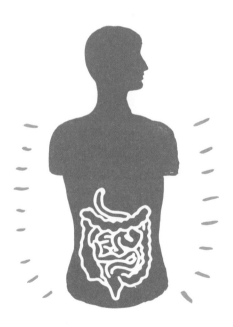

Sleep

All life on the planet has adapted itself to the constantly alternating day and night. From the smallest microbe to the largest elephant, we all have a built-in biological clock. And in fact we don't have only one but rather lots of small clocks spread out through different organs which are synchronised with the sunlight via a centre in the brain.

The bacteria in the stomach are thus controlled not by the sunlight but by the food which is offered. After breakfast, one set of bacteria flourish, and after dinner another one. And it has also been shown that the gut microbes move between different workstations where they carry out different tasks at different times of day.

The daily rhythm of the gut flora affects the production of hormones that activate a number of different bodily functions in a strict order. When we age, these hormonal daily rhythms tend to get disrupted, which can lead to sleeping problems, loss of appetite, a reduced sex drive, loss of energy, a feeling of brain fog and fatigue.

A disrupted daily rhythm increases the craving for junk food through changing levels of the hormones that control feelings of hunger and satiety. In one experiment, students were flown through different time zones so that their gut flora became imbalanced. When their faeces were then transferred into mice, the mice gained weight. This is in line with the image of shift workers more often suffering from excess weight and other physical and mental health problems than people with a normal working day.

In 2018, the results from the largest observation study on this topic by far were published, showing a clear link between a disrupted daily rhythm and an increased risk of depression. The researchers had analysed data from more than 91,000 people who had worn measurement equipment to register their movements.

It's also important to help your internal stomach clock to keep time, and this is best done by eating food at the same time every day. And of course eating varied food that contains lots of fibre.

As we all know, travel disrupts our daily rhythms. Jet-lag means that an imbalance arises between the light registered by the eyes and sent to the brain and the lagging time count in our internal organs.

Often, your internal clock's shift is made worse when you travel because you eat more processed junk food than normal with very little fibre and a lot of fat and sugar, and at all times of day and night. This makes your bad microbes take over entirely, causing you to feel even worse.

So next time you travel, enlist the aid of your gut bacteria in advance and start eating breakfast, lunch and dinner at the right time for the time zone you're visiting.

Food is more important than exercise for the gut flora

Exercise is good in almost all ways, but is it also beneficial for the gut flora? As long as you exercise, you don't need to worry about what you eat – or so we often hear. But there are surprisingly few results that support that claim.

One of the most well known is an Irish study of rugby players. These elite sportsmen, who exercised hard, turned out to have a better and more varied gut flora than people in the control group who were sedentary and ate junk food.

Case closed? No. The problem

with the study was that the rugby players also ate much better and had a more varied diet than the control group, so perhaps it was all down to the food. People who exercise a lot also tend to eat more, and this can give the gut bacteria more fibre to work with, but isn't automatically the answer – because the person's eating habits must also be good!

Other studies show that both physical and mental stress can damage the gut flora. When elite soldiers in the Norwegian Brigade Nord were exposed to extreme physical challenges during a four-day ski trek over open terrain, their gut leakage increased by 62%.

Samples of the soldiers' faeces after the ski trek turned out to contain more harmful bacteria and less of those that usually dominate any healthy gut.

One conclusion was that the problem could be reduced if the soldiers were served fibre-rich food before such physical effort.

In animal testing, researchers can see that the gut flora changes during physical activity and becomes more varied. But on a closer look, it often turns out that just like the Norwegian soldiers, the bacteria that usually constitute a stable core decrease, while those that increase can be those you don't actually want more of.

Research results recently showed that the gut flora in slim people reacted positively to endurance training, while the changes in overweight people weren't anything like as good. This would indicate that exercise works best for those who already have a healthy digestion, but not as well for those whose digestion is already disturbed. But here too, the slim people already ate a more fibre-rich diet than those who were overweight.

The conclusion is that it's really not easy to say that exercise is a quick fix for the gut flora. There's far too little research and what there is points in different directions. In the best case, the positive impact of exercise on the gut flora is neither significant nor persistent, and nor does it seem to apply equally to everyone.

There are lots of things that have to fall into place in a healthy lifestyle: food, exercise, friends, a feeling of meaningfulness, the right amount of stress, good sleep, fresh air, clean water, self-esteem and so on. All of this also affects our gut bacteria, but food seems to be the most important thing, and the one we can most easily affect.

Your exercise results quite simply depend more on your gut bacteria than the other way around.

Stress

As we have seen, physical stress in the case of hard exercise can damage the gut flora, but social stress can also have the same effect.

In one study, faecal samples were taken from students at the start of the exam term and at the end. It turned out that after studying hard, the students had fewer healthy bacteria and more pro-inflammatory bacteria.

This is due to a process that begins with the brain's hypothalamus activating a flight or fight mechanism with the help of stress hormones. The body has the rather simplistic view that stress situations are always a matter of life and death, and reacts by declaring a state of emergency.

In the short term, this leads to anxiety and to the body de-prioritising gut function and trying to get rid of the gut contents, which can lead to diarrhoea and vomiting. The more long-term biological functions that are de-prioritised include the gut's immune system, which leads to an increased opportunity for pathogenic bacteria to penetrate the gut's protective mucosa and cause inflammation.

From the start, anxiety is part of the stress reaction, but it can also be reinforced by pro-inflammatory bacteria and create an evil circle in which everyday stress makes us particularly sensitive to infections.

In laboratory tests, researchers can also see that a number of stress hormones, particularly noradrenaline, act as fertilisers for toxin-producing gut bacteria such as E. coli and salmonella. In one experiment, E. coli bacteria increased 10,000 fold in contact with stress hormones.

Conflicts with other people are also stressful and rarely good for the gut flora. American researchers recently reported astonishing results from tests on guinea pigs. Guinea pigs are very suitable for social experiments, because when two of them are brought together, they must immediately decide which of them has the higher rank.

One theory was that the guinea pig forced to be subordinate would experience the most stress, and this turned out to be true, but the difference was unexpectedly small compared to stress experienced by the victor. Both guinea pigs' gut flora was disturbed by the conflict.

But the most astonishing finding was that certain sorts of bacteria in the gut flora were more common from the start in the subordinate guinea pigs, while other bacteria dominated amongst the higher status guinea pig.

Obviously, these tests involved guinea pigs and not people, but the results indicate that the gut flora contributed right from the start to some test subjects being winners and others losers in the social pecking order. That's pretty surprising, isn't it?! Imagine if there was a leadership bacteria. If so, who is it that has the power: the MD or their microbes?

Perfect poo 2.0

There are easy ways to get answers to complicated questions. Medicine men and women have known this for thousands of years. In *Happy Food*, we gave you a basic course in poo analysis. We learned that the weight and consistency are very important. After 24 years' field work in Uganda, one of the pioneers of fibre research, British doctor Denis Burkitt, summarised his experience by saying that countries where people produce more quantities of poo need big hospitals. In Uganda, upwards of half a kilo was produced during a normal visit to the toilet, while our fibre-poor Western food means that many of us are below the limit of 225 grams per day where there's a rapid increase in the risk of colon cancer.

In *Happy Food For Life*, we want to take a closer look at colour, shape and transit time – factors that are all interlinked.

To a great extent, transit time – in other words the time it takes for a piece of food to travel in at your mouth and out at the other end – reveals the type of bacteria that dominate in your gut. Why is this? Well, if you think about a sewage pipe where there's a rapid flow, the bacteria that thrive most are those that a) manage to hang onto the walls and b) can increase very quickly.

In a sewage pipe where the content is almost stagnant, the bacteria that thrive are those that require a little longer to grow and which aren't as good at hanging onto the walls.

Based on this, it's logical for there to be more different species in a pipe where the flow is moving slowly. And the slower the flow, the more viscous the contents are, with the result that the faeces become harder. The best poo has a soft but cohesive consistency which isn't too watery or so hard that cracks are formed.

In older people – and also in some younger ones, actually – things can sometimes move very slowly. This can lead to blockages in the pipe, and in such situations pro-inflammatory bacteria thrive extremely well.

The best situation is when it moves sufficiently quickly – in other words not too fast or too slow and where there's a sufficiently soft consistency.

So what's the ideal? This is a balancing act, but a reasonably fast transit time of at least one and at most two days seems to be preferable. If it's too slow, the majority of the fibre in the food will completely ferment at the start of the colon, which means that the healthy butyric acid doesn't reach the immune cells further down in the colon. And what about the colour? Well, that directly reflects the transit time. The colour comes from the yellow bile. If you've changed a nappy on a baby, you know exactly what we're talking

about. During breastfeeding, the food quickly passes through the gut, and the poo is very yellow and smells sweetish. This is because the gut bacteria aren't able to break down the bile completely. When the process gets going and the speed reduces a little, the colour is more greenish. And when the child moves on to solid food, the transit time stabilises and the colour becomes brown. And that's when it really starts to smell bad.

Other unusual colours can be a warning signal. White can indicate an infection, while red – and particularly black – on repeated occasions, can indicate bleeding.

Test your transit time:
1. Eat cooked beetroot or drink beetroot juice.
2. Note how long it takes before your poo is red.

In the best of worlds, this takes about 36 hours. Other ways to test your transit time are to swallow whole sweetcorn kernels and then keep an eye on the loo.

You can shorten a long transit time by adding things like wheat bran to your diet. A short transit time with loose poo can be extended by eating soluble fibre that binds the excess liquid. This can be found in foods such as apples.

Waldorf salad

A classic created in the 1890s, but one of the cornerstones of the dish – celery – was known long before that for its healing properties. Celery is rich in quercetin and kaempferol, which are thought to provide protection against depression caused by stress. Celery also contains strong anti-inflammatory substances that are used in Chinese medicine for gout and rheumatism.

100g Roquefort cheese
1–2 frisée lettuce
2 sour apples, e.g. Granny Smith
2 sticks of celery
100g walnuts
small pinch of salt
1 lemon
3 tablespoons olive oil

1. Place the cheese in the freezer for about one hour (it needn't be fully frozen).
2. Pick out the fine, young, light leaves of the lettuce, rinse in cold water and dry in a salad spinner or on kitchen paper.
3. Slice one of the apples thinly (2–3mm), stack the slices and slice again into thin strips.
4. Peel the celery and slice into strips like the apples.
5. Dry roast the walnuts over a medium-high heat, then leave to cool.
6. Coarsely grate the remaining apple, add salt and squeeze over the juice of the lemon.
7. Sieve the grated apple and lemon juice, squeezing out all of the fruit juice.
8. Whisk the fruit juice and add the oil a little at a time to make a vinaigrette.
9. To serve, mix the lettuce, apple, celery and vinaigrette.
10. Crush the walnuts over the salad and then grate the cheese over the dish with the coarse side of the grater.

Spinach omelette with sheep's milk cheese and pine nuts

An omelette is like a blank page that can be filled with … spinach, sheep's milk cheese and pine nuts? Mmm. Perfect for breakfast or brunch, or almost any time of the day.

6 eggs
2 tablespoons water
small pinch of salt
2 tablespoons butter
1 large handful of spinach, rinsed
2 tablespoons grated pecorino
3 tablespoons toasted pine nuts
grated raw carrot or shredded
   cabbage for serving, if required

1. Whisk together the eggs, water and salt.
2. Heat a frying pan over a medium-high heat.
3. Add half the butter and allow to melt.
4. Pour the egg mixture into the pan. As the omelette solidifies, gently raise the edges with a spatula so that the egg mixture runs down.
5. Fry the spinach in the remaining butter in a hot pan for 30–40 seconds, or until soft.
6. Place the spinach on one half of the omelette and sprinkle over the cheese and pine nuts.
7. Carefully fold the other half of the omelette over the spinach.
8. Serve with grated raw carrot or shredded cabbage.

Tomato dip with sourdough bread and olive oil

This is a delicious tomato dip spiced up with a splash of vinegar. It's perfect as a starter, for example on a bruschetta, or as a side dish with soup or pasta. Make sure the tomatoes are ripe.

500g sweet and ripe tomatoes
3 shallots
1 clove of garlic
4 tablespoons olive oil
2 tablespoons red wine vinegar
1 red chilli
6–8 basil leaves, wood sorrel
  or herb of your choice
salt

1. Cut the tomatoes in half and roughly chop or grate the cut surface coarsely with a grater (hold the tomato by the skin).
2. Add salt and suspend in a fine sieve for approximately one hour. If you grated the tomatoes you will obtain a thick consistency.
3. Finely chop the shallots and garlic and quickly fry without allowing them to brown in a hot pan with 1 teaspoon of the olive oil.
4. Mix with the tomato mixture, the remaining olive oil and red wine vinegar and season with salt.
5. Halve the chilli and remove the seeds.
6. Shred the basil leaves, sorrel or chosen herbs.
7. Top the tomato dip with chilli and herbs.
8. Serve with freshly toasted sourdough bread (page 206) or roast chicken breast with grilled salad (page 122).

EMOTIONAL EATING

CHAPTER 6.

Infectious emotions

Can the global epidemic of mental illness largely be exactly that – an infectious epidemic?
No matter how unlikely this may sound, there are strong indications that this is the case.

If you don't fancy reading about gastroenteritis, but would prefer to flick forward a few pages to Niklas' tasty recipes, here's the top tip before you go: reinforce your defences by eating fibre-rich food such as beans, onions, cabbage, leafy green vegetables and whole grains. Top it all off with fruit, berries, seeds and nuts. And if you eat meat, make sure it comes from animals that have been raised humanely. There's a simple rule of thumb: you can't feel better than the food you eat did!

Here's a spot of investigative food reportage in the middle of the cookery bit. There seems to be an important cause of the bowel disease IBS and mental illness that both the authorities and the majority of researchers have missed. Even Niklas and I were astonished when we realised what our survey indicated.

Against the background of the rapid increase in and the strong co-morbidities between mental illness and bowel diseases, together with a long list of other chronic diseases, an entirely new image is appearing – one that's previously been completely unknown to the general public. These epidemics have gained speed in recent decades, in parallel with our own immune systems being depleted, which is reflected in a reduced number of species in the gut.

In May 2000, more than 2,300 inhabitants of the small Canadian town of Walkerton fell ill with gastroenteritis, in a tragedy that killed six people and left many others with permanent illness.

An unusual amount of rain had fallen and large areas had flooded, including some of the farms in the area. Manure leaked into the drinking water supply, infecting it with campylobacter and toxic E. coli bacteria of type O157:H7 – also known as EHEC. This bacteria had appeared from nowhere a few years earlier and spread across the world.

Campylobacter has existed for many years and is found particularly in birds. The bacteria thrives in the large intensive farms that raise thousands of chickens for meat and eggs in a very small area. The bacteria is also sometimes found in the guts of pigs.

Gastrointestinal infections caused by campylobacter are the most common form of food poisoning in the Western world, and the primary reason why public health authorities encourage us to heat poultry thoroughly and to use different knives and cutting boards for each type of foodstuff.

Six months after the outbreak of gastroenteritis in Walkerton, the town's doctor noticed a stream of patients complaining of stomach problems. It soon became apparent that hundreds of inhabitants had been affected by the chronic inflammatory bowel disease IBS. The symptoms first appeared several months after they had recovered from the acute gastroenteritis.

Often, outbreaks of gastrointestinal infection caused by aggressive gut bacteria are hard to follow up, because those who are affected live over a wide area and fall ill on different occasions. And mental illness and stomach problems are treated by completely different doctors. But in Walkerton, almost half of the population fell ill at the same time, and the pattern was suddenly clear. This represented a golden opportunity for researchers, and a major project was inaugurated to follow up the population's health.

The link between gastroenteritis and the subsequent development of chronic gut problems was astonishing but not entirely unexpected. During the Second World War, the same connection had already been noticed among British soldiers affected by dysentery.

After that, a handful of smaller studies had shown that between 4 and 32% of those who develop a gastrointestinal infection later develop IBS. But the field was difficult to study: the patients had been followed up only over a relatively short period, and entirely different bacteria had been involved.

The risks were better known to veterinarians. Perhaps because chronic gut problems in animals cost a lot of money in the form of poorer growth.

Soon the first research results from Walkerton began to arrive. It turned out that from three to six months after the outbreak, one in five people who had contracted gastroenteritis developed IBS.

Following up this outbreak of food poisoning – the most

extensive in Canada's history –
was to continue for over a decade.
Two years after the outbreak, one
in four (28.3%) of those who had
been infected by the drinking
water – and who had not previously
suffered from bowel problems – had
developed IBS.

Researchers already knew that
both IBS and other inflammatory
bowel diseases are related to an
increased risk of anxiety and
depression. The co-morbidity rate
is usually between 30 and 50%.

In Walkerton, researchers could
use medical records and interviews
with patients to identify those who
had suffered from chronic bowel
problems and mental illness before
the outbreak. Both the researchers
and ordinary healthcare personnel
then noted a clear increase in
mental problems among those who
had previously been healthy, but
the results were not included in the
study and were never published.

The link between IBS and
mental illness is two-
directional. This means
that those who suffer from
anxiety or depression are
more easily affected by
chronic gut problems. But the
opposite seems to be even
more common: that chronic
stomach problems trigger
poor mental health.

Here, the actual inflammation
is a decisive factor. We'll look at
exactly how in a later chapter.

The results from Walkerton are
extremely useful. In the USA, the
infection authority CDC (Centers
for Disease Control and Prevention)
estimates that one in six Americans
– or 48 million people – are affected
by food poisoning every year. If the
figures from Walkerton turn out
to be representative, this would
give an entirely new and important
explanation for millions of cases
every year of both chronic bowel
problems and mental illness. And
not just in the USA, but across the
entire world. And yet this is very
rarely named in the debate about
mental illness.

It would perhaps have been
possible to brush aside the example
of Walkerton, except for the fact
that we soon encountered other
similar cases. In the Norwegian
city of Bergen, another waterborne outbreak occurred in 2004,
this time caused by the parasite
Giardia. This is a common cause
of traveller's diarrhoea, not least
in India and Nepal, which many
people are affected by on holiday.

Researchers at the University
of Bergen noted that many of those
affected complained about stomach
pain that appeared after they
had recovered from the Giardia
infection, so the researchers took

the opportunity to follow up what happened with those who had been infected. The first study showed that 12 to 30 months after the outbreak, more than 80% had some form of IBS symptoms.

Six years after the Norwegian outbreak the researchers observed that almost four in ten of those infected (291 out of 748) who had previously been healthy had fully developed IBS.

And almost as many had been affected by chronic fatigue syndrome. Here, no distinction was made between fatigue syndrome and the diseases ME/CFS, which is sometimes called chronic fatigue syndrome. ME/CFS, which is often a life-long disease, almost always occurs after a gut infection such as flu or traveller's diarrhoea.

The risk of being affected by both IBS and fatigue syndrome was up to eight times higher among those who had been infected by Giardia six years earlier than for those in a control group of people who had not been infected.

The risk of permanent problems was also greatest among those who had been most sick and who had been treated with antibiotics. The researchers who followed up the outbreak drew the conclusion that IBS and what is classified as fatigue syndrome, where some symptoms resemble depression, can have

several causes but often appear to be related to gut bacteria of a type that many people are exposed to during foreign holidays.

In 2018 a new follow up study was carried out which showed that ten years after the outbreak in Bergen, four in ten of those infected were still suffering from IBS. However, the proportion who also suffered from fatigue syndrome had dropped from 40 to 25%.

'When we first saw the results that showed 40% had developed IBS and chronic fatigue syndrome, we were astonished and thought that nobody would believe us. There was simply nothing in the literature about this,' says Nina Langeland, professor in infectious diseases at the University of Bergen.

It seems to be only the outbreaks in Bergen and in Walkerton that have been properly followed up, and I ask Nina Langeland how this can be the case, given that gastrointestinal infections and mental illness are so common.

'I think it's fascinating too. Major outbreaks are quite rare and are often only followed up over the short term by authorities, and then the researchers analyse the microbes in laboratories. To even begin to study this you have to go out and meet the patients and realise that there's a pattern where an unexpectedly large number of people are complaining of tiredness and stomach problems despite having recovered from the initial infection,' explains Nina Langeland. 'The results from Walkerton seem to agree completely with ours. I believe that these problems can occur as a consequence of many different bacteria and parasites that cause bowel infections. But what we'd like to know is why some people are affected more severely than others.'

One more known outbreak has been studied. Nina Langeland describes the well known case in Germany in 2011, during which several people died after eating bean sprouts containing toxic E. coli bacteria. A small-scale follow up study showed that 19 months after the outbreak, 22 out of 31 investigated patients suffered from chronic tiredness, headaches and concentration difficulties. The symptoms had recurred in a second wave after the patients had initially recovered.

We can add to this a recent study carried out on American soldiers, which showed that to the same high level, IBS was a consequence of other common gut parasites in addition to Giardia.

The pattern which has become evident is so clear that it feels rather improbable that it could have remained undetected for so long.

But the few researchers who have studied this subject seem to have been quite spread out and relatively isolated, without significant contact with each other.

I have also found researchers who warn that even significantly less serious infections than those that occurred in Bergen and Walkerton can trigger similar symptoms. In December 2017, an American group reported that during animal testing, they had discovered that repeated small infections by salmonella bacteria could gradually break down the gut defences.

On each occasion, the food poisoning was so minor that it almost went unnoticed, but it still wiped out production of the enzyme the body uses to break down the toxin produced by the bacteria.

The alarming conclusion that these researchers reached was that repeated, extremely minor food poisoning seems to be able to start a chain of events that ultimately results in severe inflammatory bowel diseases.

In Walkerton, the researchers took faecal samples from the inhabitants suffering from IBS. It turned out that their gut flora was damaged and unbalanced. They then tested transferring the faecal matter to mice, with the result that the mice showed signs of increased anxiety.

The fact that mental illness can't merely be triggered by aggressive bacteria and imbalances in the gut flora, but that it's even possible to transfer it with a transplant of faecal matter – at least from people to mice – was something that, at the time, completely took researchers by surprise.

But it shouldn't be so astonishing that bacteria can cause mental symptoms. The bacteria that causes syphilis came to Europe with no less than Christopher Columbus when he returned from America. The symptoms were horrifying at the start, with ulcers all over the body that soon began to rot before the patients were finally released from their suffering by death.

But bacteria so toxic that the patient dies immediately are sabotaging their own survival. They hamper their own opportunities to spread further. Over time, the syphilis bacterium mutated so that it became slightly less deadly, but became instead the first bacterium known to cause mental illness. The cure only arrived with the discovery of antibiotics.

Nearly ten years ago, I wrote a book about how bacteria such as campylobacter, E. coli and salmonella had developed over just a few decades to become much more aggressive and infectious. One of the people who introduced me to the subject was the well known professor of nutrition and microbiologist Marion Nestle, at New York University, who explained how modern large-scale intensive animal breeding has become a perfect hothouse environment for rapid development of infectious bacteria and viruses.

Modern livestock farms constitute an environment with many genetically similar cows, pigs and chickens, which are bred and raised for maximum fast growth, which produces animals with fragile immune systems. A bacterium couldn't ask for better conditions for mutating.

In many cases, they have mutated into new variants which are more toxic and which spread more quickly and in new ways. In other words, this is independent of the fact that we also have rapidly increasing antibiotic resistance. This is the price we have to pay for mass production of cheap meat.

There are many examples, such as salmonella which first mutated in the early 1970s, allowing the bacteria to travel through egg shells. Or EHEC, which was completely unknown until the 1980s. Then it appeared from nowhere and caused a deadly outbreak in food sold by an American hamburger chain. Today, EHEC has spread through cattle all over the world.

How can we combine nutrition with enjoyment?

Hang on a minute! In the previous chapter we were encouraged to eat soil and not to be too hung up about hygiene. But now we discover that gastroenteritis bacteria create serious and long-term problems. How does that make sense?

Quite right. There's a dilemma here. We can't pretend that we are surrounded by an environment in perfect balance like an indigenous tribe in the Amazon where the children can eat soil without risks.

As I wrote in the previous chapter, we need to reinforce our immune systems by enriching our gut flora. But this also requires common sense, and a certain amount of vigilance to avoid contaminants. In the long-term, we need to create stable ecosystems in our surroundings, and not least in the entire food chain. And we need to think differently to achieve this.

For 100 years, our only strategy has been to hunt down bacteria. This has been done through improved hygiene, and also with the help of antibiotics and other forms of sterilisation that get rid of all bacteria – good and bad.

The point of having a strong immune system is obvious. If we have a sound gut, thousands of salmonella bacteria are required to make us sick, but if the intestinal mucosa are damaged, just a few are enough to infect us. So one answer is the theme that permeates this book – eating a varied and fibre-rich diet that reinforces your own microbial home guard. Another answer is of course to follow the authorities' advice: to rinse vegetables, use different knives for each type of food, and to store cold and hot food properly.

But the best thing would be if the responsibility for food safety was shifted away from the consumer's own kitchen and back out to the farms. Because the problem can be solved there too, with good animal protection rules, biological diversity and farmers who actually get paid for high standards where the animals are healthy and toxic bacteria can't thrive.

This would require many different types of effort, one of which would be to return to older animal breeds with greater genetic differences and which grow a little more slowly – but which are also healthier and more resistant as a result. And the need for antibiotics would also reduce into the bargain.

Somebody always pays the price for cheap meat. Most often it's the animal, but my study also shows that the price we pay ourselves has become unexpectedly high and may have contributed to the current epidemic of mental illness.

The art of killing bacteria

Niklas and I don't like killing bacteria unnecessarily. But to reduce the risk of bacteria such as campylobacter and EHEC in meat, it's sometimes necessary.

Remember that this is a matter of both temperature and time. If the meat is heated to 75°C, as many bacteria die in one second as during 15 minutes at 65°C. Aim for around 70°C. Beefburgers must be heated particularly carefully because the bacteria which were initially on the surface can now also be in the middle.

Happy Food For Life – Part 1.

Fact: Depression

According to new calculations presented by the World Health Organisation in 2017, depression is the leading cause of illness and disability in the world. More than 300 million people suffer from depression – an increase of 18% between 2005 and 2015 – and one in six people is affected at some point in their life.

There's a strong connection between depression and a long list of other diseases, and with drug and medication addiction – and even suicide.

According to the WHO, depression increases the risk of cardiovascular disease and diabetes, and the opposite also applies: people with these diseases have an increased risk of suffering from depression.

Parkinson's, Alzheimer's, the bowel diseases IBS and IBD, obesity, psoriasis, MS, autism and many others also increase the risk of depression.

Common symptoms of depression are a lack of energy, reduced appetite, sleeping too much or too little, difficulties concentrating, a feeling of indecision, restlessness, feeling worthless, feeling guilt and hopelessness and even thoughts of suicide or self-harm.

What on earth is
a leaky gut?

It's time to get out the magnifying glass and take a closer look at what happens when we get gastroenteritis. The cell walls of gastroenteritis bacteria contain a toxin called endotoxin. This is found in many bacteria, but it is the quantity and strength that differentiates a pathogenic bacteria from others.

This toxin is what's known as an antigen, which triggers our immune system. The toxin can also paralyse the cells in our own gut wall so that they don't divide, which contributes to what we call leaky gut. Suddenly, the gaps between the cells in the extremely thin gut wall become a little larger.

Normally, fine food molecules would pass through these gaps as part of the natural food absorption process, but now it's possible for slightly larger than normal molecules to squeeze through.

When the toxin can also penetrate the gut wall, our immune cells become activated and even at small doses cause measurable inflammation which can become chronic. This can make us feel ill,

but it can also carry on relatively unnoticed over a long time and can ultimately cause a range of other diseases.

We know this because in 2001, researchers injected people with such low doses of endotoxins that they didn't cause gastroenteritis. But even very low doses turned out to be able to trigger transient episodes of anxiety and depression.

In other words, we seem to be going through a perfect storm that benefits the development of chronic inflammation and related diseases, such as mental illness. At exactly the same time that our protective gut flora is depleted by repetitive, fibre-poor Western food, just the type of bacteria that we particularly nourish with such food have not merely increased but have also become more toxic. And these bacteria can start a chain that leads to anxiety and depression.

How to protect yourself in two easy steps

With a healthy gut flora that you nourish with varied, fibre-rich food, you can tolerate more gastroenteritis bacteria without becoming ill.

And if you eat meat, make sure that it comes from healthy animals who haven't spent large parts of their life squeezed into small spaces.

Stomach ache

Irritable Bowel Syndrome (IBS) is a very common cause of gut problems that affect 10–15% of the population, and most often women. IBS was once considered to be non-inflammatory, but in recent years it has been shown to be associated with low-grade inflammation.

Inflammatory Bowel Disease (IBD) is a collective name for several diseases with clear chronic inflammation in the gut wall or the intestinal mucosa. The two most common are Crohn's disease and ulcerative colitis.

There are high levels of co-morbidity between a number of other diseases and conditions and IBS/IBD. These include ME/chronic fatigue syndrome, but also autism.

An ancient motorway from the stomach to the brain

Nature has programmed us to lie low when we have an infection. This is a clever solution that probably developed to force us to rest and gather our energy, but also to prevent us from spreading the infection.

We are also very quick and accurate at detecting the subtle signs that show someone has fallen ill – paler skin, drooping mouth and eyelids and a slightly hunched posture. And many animals can smell disease.

Our reaction to gastroenteritis is regulated by the immune system, which doesn't merely attack aggressive gastroenteritis bacteria, but also uses signal substances known as cytokines to inform the brain that it's time to feel tired, feverish and lethargic.

How your gut bacteria affect your emotions

Step 1. You start to feel slightly nauseous and apprehensive. What's happening is that your friendly gut bacteria are attacking the unwelcome visitors. Cells in the gut wall sound the alarm by secreting the signal substance serotonin, which makes the muscles around the gut contract and perhaps causes it to rumble alarmingly. Then the signal substances travel up to the brain via the vagus nerve. This makes you feel slight discomfort.

Step 2. After one or two days, you begin to be really ill with diarrhoea. This is a sign that your own immune system has got up steam. More serotonin is secreted, making the stomach contract with cramps. At the same time, the immune system sprays out cytokines, which warn immune cells throughout the body of the danger. Now the immune system is in top gear. The battle must be won, even if some of the body's own cells become casualties of war. Fever and a headache make you feel wretched.

Step 3. Your hormonal system is activated throughout what is known as the HPA axis or stress axis. Initially, the immune system's cytokines send out substances that dampen the production of dopamine, serotonin and noradrenaline, and even the thyroid hormone thyroxine. This contributes to you feeling sick, depressed and lacking energy. After some time, the secretion of the stress hormone cortisol increases, which helps to dampen the immune system so that it reacts proportionally to the number of attacking bacteria. One side-effect of cortisol is that it can trigger anxiety.

It is therefore considered that a low-grade chronic inflammation can result in persistent low levels of signal substances such as noradrenaline, dopamine and serotonin, which all affect our health and well-being in different ways. Noradrenaline affects wakefulness, activity and attention, and low levels are associated with depression. Dopamine plays a central role in the reward system, while serotonin affects everything from sleep and appetite to mood and well-being. The information also means constant production of anxiety-producing stress hormones.

Spicy tomato soup with lentils

Tomato soup often brings back childhood memories. It's also full of fibre and healthy substances. And the lycopene in the tomatoes is also good for the prostate.

1 red chilli
3 shallots
3 cloves of garlic
2 tablespoons olive oil
1 tablespoon coriander seeds
1 tablespoon fennel seeds
800ml tomato juice
200ml water
300g cooked green lentils
2–3 tablespoons lemon juice
6–8 celery leaves/fresh
   coriander for topping
salt

1. Halve the chilli and remove the seeds.
2. Peel and slice the shallots and garlic.
3. Fry the chilli, shallots and garlic over a medium-high heat in olive oil without allowing them to brown (1–2 minutes).
4. Add the coriander and fennel seeds and continue to fry for a few minutes.
5. Add the tomato juice and water, bring to the boil and simmer for 20 minutes.
6. Add the lentils.
7. Season with salt and lemon juice and top with celery leaves to serve.

Socca – chickpea pancake with rocket, feta and olive oil

Socca is a traditional dish with its roots in Provence, but which spread to Liguri, Italy. Chickpeas contain good fibre for the gut and you can vary the garnish almost endlessly.

200g chickpea flour
4 tablespoons olive oil
½ teaspoon salt
250ml water
1 bunch of rocket
100g feta cheese
small pinch of black pepper,
   freshly ground
2 tablespoons olive oil for serving

1. Whisk together the chickpea flour, olive oil, salt and water until you have a smooth batter.
2. Leave to stand for 1 hour at room temperature (add a little more water if necessary to obtain a runny consistency).
3. Preheat the oven to 220°C.
4. Oil a pie dish (or cast iron pan 25–30cm in diameter) with olive oil. Pour in the batter.
5. Place in the oven and bake for 12–15 minutes until the batter has set and browned a little.
6. Remove from the oven and top with rocket, crumbled feta, freshly ground black pepper and olive oil.

Socca – chickpea pancake
with rocket, feta and olive
oil (see page 95)

Raw Savoy salad with avocado, chilli and buckwheat

The buckwheat in this delicious salad actually isn't a cereal at all, but is instead a relative of rhubarb. Naturally gluten-free, buckwheat also contains high levels of magnesium, which many people are short of, and fibre that helps the gut bacteria feel good. The best way to avoid developing intolerances is not to eat a monotonous diet. Vary what you eat!

100g crushed buckwheat
3 tablespoons oil for frying
1 Savoy cabbage
2 red chillies
2 avocados
1 lime
salt

1. Soak the buckwheat in plenty of cold water in the fridge for 8 hours, or ideally overnight.
2. Drain the buckwheat in a sieve and continue to rinse with cold water until the water is clear and the starch has been removed. Leave in the sieve to drain thoroughly.
3. Fry the buckwheat in oil until golden brown and crisp over a medium-high heat in a frying pan. Fry in 2–3 batches. Place on kitchen paper to drain.
4. Remove the outermost leaves of the Savoy cabbage if they are woody or damaged.
5. Shred thinly into 4–5mm strips, and rinse in cold water. Dry in a salad spinner or leave to drain on kitchen paper.
6. Mix the cabbage with 1 teaspoon of salt and knead until it releases liquid, the cabbage darkens and becomes easier to chew (if it's too salty, rinse it in cold water then dry off on kitchen paper or with a salad spinner).
7. Halve the chillies lengthways and remove the seeds. Finely chop the chillies.
8. Open the avocados, remove the stones and cut into rough cubes.
9. Mix the avocado, chilli and shredded Savoy cabbage. Squeeze the lime juice over and season with more salt if required.
10. Crush the toasted buckwheat and sprinkle over the salad.

HAPTER 7.

From fish fats to fibre

For modern science, it has been a long and winding road to the conclusion that the stomach and well-being are related. Let's take a short trip back in time to follow that journey.

In 1972, British researcher Michael Crawford concluded that Omega-3 fats were very important for brain development. Other researchers soon reported about the link between a lack of healthy fish fats and mental illness.

At the end of the 20th century, the focus was on investigating whether different vitamins and minerals could affect our mental health. A range of exciting results were published relating to zinc and magnesium.

Around the turn of the millennium, the vitamin D debate was launched in earnest, and it soon became clear that the sunshine vitamin doesn't merely give stronger bones but can also have an inhibitory effect on depression and other mental illness. What we didn't then know was that vitamin D also contributes to a richer and more well-balanced gut flora.

Reports stated that folate also seemed to have an inhibiting effect on depression. Folate is found above all in liver and other offal – but also in beans and leafy green vegetables.

But supplements aren't enough for anyone who eats poorly overall, so the focus was aimed at the effects of the diet as a whole. Now the breakthrough wasn't far off. In 2009 and 2010, three articles were published in prestigious journals referring to large-scale observation studies, in which people had been interviewed about their eating habits and which showed that there is a link between food and mental health. However, this type of study could not say with certainty whether there was also a causal relationship. An alternative explanation could be that you eat worse when you feel bad.

In the first study, researchers who examined 3,486 middle-aged Londoners reported that the risk of being affected by depression within five years was significantly increased for those eating a lot of sugary, greasy and fried junk food. Conversely, the Londoners who instead ate a lot of vegetables were protected against depression to a greater degree.

At around the same time, the results of a Norwegian study showed that a Western diet with a lot of junk food increased the risk of depression, while a traditional Scandinavian low processed diet with meat, fish, vegetables and whole grains reduced the risk of both anxiety and depression. A large Spanish study also showed corresponding results for a traditional Mediterranean diet.

During the next few years, similar results were published from many other observation studies, but contradictory results were also published – which is logical. Nobody believes that food causes all mental illness. Increasing numbers of researchers are now taking an interest in the link between chronic inflammation and depression.

Today, cardiovascular disease is clearly linked to such information. People affected by cardiovascular disease also run an increased risk of depression. A logical next step was then to investigate whether the Mediterranean diet – with its demonstrated preventative effect on both cardiovascular disease and inflammation – could also have an anti-depressive effect.

It turned out that it could, and now researchers around the world began to go back to their data and investigate the impact of food on the mental health of the large majority – in various studies at least one third of all those with depression – who showed signs of increased inflammation.

An index was developed that estimated how much different ingredients contributed to or counteracted inflammation. Over and over again, the answer was that the protective effect of food was strongest when people with depression also suffered from increased inflammation.

The index has since then been tested with the world's largest observation studies, including the Harvard studies Nurses' Health Study and Women's Health Initiative. Other examples are the Spanish Predimed and the British Whitehall II, which in the 1990s contributed to knocking the final nail into the coffin of tobacco smoking.

But we were still lacking experimental studies that could resolve the remaining uncertainties in terms of cause and effect. Is it the fault of junk food that someone is depressed, or do depressed people eat more junk food? The answer seems to be both, but junk food generally comes first.

In 2017, the results were published of the first experimental study into the effect of food on severe depression. The study was carried out in Australia, and the question the researchers asked was: what happens if we give dietary advice to patients suffering from the disease?

The food that was prescribed was the Mediterranean diet with slightly less meat than normal, but reinforced with extra olive oil and nuts. Exactly the type of food that seemed to give such good effects in previous Spanish studies.

The result: after 12 weeks, one third of participants had recovered so much that they no longer fulfilled the criteria for the diagnosis. This is a result comparable to that from many medications, but this time completely without side-effects.

The Mediterranean diet also had a positive effect on less serious symptoms such as irritation, fatigue and lack of initiative.

The Australian study, which was baptised SMILES, wasn't very big and there was quite a high drop out rate among those in the control group who didn't get dietary advice. So the study needed to be followed up by others.

In December 2017, the results of another Australian experimental study, entitled Helfimed, were published. This was twice as big, and the researchers had produced very similar, and actually slightly better, results than the previous Australian study.

But that's only half of the story. In the meantime, other researchers had made major progress when it came to determining in the lab exactly what role our gut flora play in how well we feel. And here, too, changes had been observed in the gut flora of those suffering from depression.

When all of the pieces were put together, the picture really began to come clear.

The only side effect:
You live for longer!

Food can help you to feel healthy and alert. But it can also help you to stay healthy and, apparently, in many cases bring relief. From lab trials to large dietary studies, and even in a number of small and medium experimental studies, the findings point in one direction: the food we eat has a crucial impact on our well-being. But how strong is the evidence?

In summer 2017, researchers from all over the world gathered in the town of Bethesda near Washington, D.C., for the first international conference held by the newly formed network ISNPR, the International Society for Nutrition and Psychiatric Research.

This was a unique event. The world's leading experts within two areas of knowledge that had previously run along parallel tracks came together for the first time.

On one side: the researchers who had explored the link between the food we eat and our mental health long before the gut bacteria became a focus for research.

On the other side: the people who had more recently made pioneering discoveries when it came to mapping the role played by our gut bacteria, how they are connected to our brains and how they affect our emotions.

When these groups came together to review the results of many different types of study, the conclusions were clear. The food we eat undoubtedly affects how we feel and there's a connection between Western junk food and mental illness. But what's still missing are the large randomised experimental studies – in other words, carefully implemented experiments with many participants.

Everyone at the conference agreed it is important for these to be carried out to completely investigate cause and effect, the patients most receptive to treatment with dietary advice, and exactly which types of food work best, regardless of whether you're healthy or sick.

But given that a global epidemic of mental illness is under way, the researchers assembled in Bethesda saw no reason to wait. They said that there was already so much convincing evidence for the positive impact of food from hundreds of reliable studies of different types that it would be irresponsible to not begin developing methods for diagnosing and treating depression with dietary advice as a complement to conventional treatment. Food must become as obvious a factor in treatment and advice as exercise.

Those attending that conference in Bethesda in summer 2017 believed that there was a simple answer to the question of food and mental health. The Mediterranean diet, but also traditional Scandinavian and Japanese food, seems to have a clear positive effect on how we feel while also lacking negative side-effects.

The only side-effects you actually run are getting a stronger heart, reducing your risk of diabetes and living for several years longer.

Avocado half with salmon and chilli

Avocado is filling and rich in healthy fats, vitamins and minerals. It also contains high levels of enzymes that help you break down the other food on the plate. Here we're adding a touch of coriander, the favourite herb in the Italian villages where some of the world's oldest people live.

2 avocados
400g good-quality salmon
1 tablespoon soy sauce
2 tablespoons sriracha sauce
2 tablespoons chopped coriander
1 tablespoon sesame seeds, toasted
1 tablespoon chopped chives

1. Cut the avocados into halves, discard the stone and scoop out the flesh. Set the skin to one side.
2. Cut the avocado flesh and salmon into approximately 1cm cubes.
3. Mix with the soy sauce, sriracha and coriander.
4. Place back in the avocado skins.
5. Top with sesame seeds and chives.

Egg halves with anchovies

Eggs are a good example of the often distorted view of food that we have today. For several hundred thousand years, eggs were a self-evident, but not always easy to find, basic foodstuff. Then they suddenly became cholesterol bombs. And then they were once again considered as healthy. So let's just calm down! We've even heard of people who eat pretty much only eggs. Moderation is always best. Go for fewer but better-quality eggs, ideally organic ones.

4 eggs
1 clove of garlic
3–5 anchovies
4 tablespoons mayonnaise
2 tablespoons crème fraîche
1 tablespoon lemon juice
2 teaspoons Dijon mustard
a pinch of paprika
2 tablespoons chopped parsley
salt

1. Place the eggs in boiling water and allow to boil for 9 minutes. Cool in iced water.
2. Shell the eggs, cut in half and remove the yolks.
3. Chop the egg yolks, grate the garlic and chop the anchovies.
4. Mix with the mayonnaise, crème fraîche, lemon juice and mustard.
5. If necessary, season with more anchovies, garlic, lemon juice and salt.
6. Pile the mixture back into the egg halves.
7. Top with paprika and chopped parsley.

Tortilla with tarragon
and poppy seeds

A potato omelette doesn't merely awaken a yearning for
Spain. It's also an easy way of using up the leftovers in
the fridge! Don't throw food away unnecessarily! A large
proportion of the world's food is actually consumed by …
the rubbish bin. That's totally insane.

6 eggs
6–8 cold boiled potatoes
8–12 mushrooms in season
2 onions
2 tablespoons butter
1 bunch of spinach
8–12 tarragon leaves
1 bunch of rocket
3 tablespoons olive oil
1 shallot
100ml crème fraîche
1 tablespoon poppy seeds
salt

1. Preheat the oven to 175°C.
2. Whisk the eggs.
3. Peel and halve the boiled
   potatoes. Wash the mushrooms
   and cut into quarters. Coarsely
   chop the onions.
4. Fry the onions and mushrooms
   in 1 tablespoon of the butter for
   2–3 minutes. Add the spinach
   and continue to fry for 1 minute
   until the spinach has wilted.
5. Mix the fried vegetables with
   the potatoes and eggs.
6. Melt the remaining tablespoon
   of butter.
7. Preheat an ovenproof dish
   or frying pan, brush with the
   melted butter and pour in the
   egg mixture.
8. Bake in the oven for 30 minutes.
9. Remove from the oven when it
   has set. Carefully lift the edges
   with a spatula and turn out
   onto a dish.
10. Mix the tarragon and rocket
    with olive oil and finely chopped
    shallot. Add a pinch of salt.
11. Drizzle crème fraîche over the
    omelette and sprinkle with
    poppy seeds. Serve the salad
    with the omelette.

MEALS THAT CHEER

Part 2.

In Part 1, we explored the gut and the effect of the bacterial flora on how we feel. Now it's time to take a closer look at food and its importance for both body and brain. We look at the meaning of cookery in human social life and the development of the human species, and how the social and nutritional composition of food reduces the risk of criminality. We also introduce the latest findings about what's known as personal nutrition, and note that traditional Scandinavian food has a lot to offer – for both your taste buds and your health!

SET FOR
SUCCESS

The fellowship of the pot

Few things have meant so much to humans as the art of cooking food. Before we learned to cook, we spent much of the day chewing. The ability to cook released more nutrients from the raw ingredients and gave us time for other things – such as building a civilisation, formulating theories and creating art. Around the cooking fire, we developed social abilities and shared both ladles and microbes.

In the first part of this book, we looked at pioneering discoveries and our current state of knowledge. In this part, we will find out how, through meals and ingredients, we can apply this knowledge – and thus become a little happier.

The starting point can seem rather dismal. The time a normal contemporary family spends on cooking food has halved in just one generation. Today, many people spend a lot more time watching cookery on TV than they do on cooking themselves.

Is this an example of our era being out of step with reality? No, not necessarily. Niklas and other TV chefs do an important job of spreading knowledge and stimulating an interest in cookery.

As Michael Pollan, one of my favourite food writers, observes, cooking has been surrounded by an aura of mysticism for thousands of years, and this current interest instead shows how deeply embedded this is in our DNA.

Pollan says that even in the Neolithic Age, most people would have probably watched while the cooks stirred the cooking pots, transforming the ingredients in an almost magical way into something more than the individual ingredients. This is also common among today's indigenous peoples.

Watching food preparation seems to bring us an inherited feeling of security, belonging and confidence in the future. With food in your stomach, you and your nearest and dearest hope to be able to survive another day.

While other primates were forced to spend up to seven hours a day chewing on various parts of plants, thanks to cooking, we could get more energy and nutrition in a considerably shorter time. Cooking freed up more time for more varied food and for hunting and fishing.

It didn't seem to be grilling over an open fire that dominated, but instead stews where meat and plants were cooked in liquid. In this way, starches could be released and the fat in the meat could be utilised while toxic substances were neutralised. Progress also made it easier to find food because more types of ingredients could be used, which also saved yet more time for our ancestors.

Cooking has existed for so long that the size of our guts has adapted to cooked food. This meant that our teeth and jaws shrank and gave us flat faces different from those of the apes. Everything seems to indicate that it was even cooking that provided our brains with the raw material that made them grow.

First we cooked food.
Then it made us healthy.

It has been estimated that people learned to control fire and started to cook their food around 1.8 million years ago. It was there, in the shift from apelike ancestors such as *Homo habilis* to the upright *Homo erectus*, that the most dramatic changes in human brain volume and other physical attributes took place. The length of their forearms and the upright position shows that *Homo erectus* could no longer seek protection in the trees. Instead, fire must have been required to keep wild animals away.

Encounters over food must also have formed us in different ways. At the same time as our brains grew, our ancestors got used to eye contact, to controlling their impulses and waiting their turn. At mealtimes, children learned to be social beings, to listen and argue calmly without offending other people and getting into fights.

Today we see the exact opposite, with people eating alone or on the run, while hate and implacability are increasing through anonymous social media.

Physical proximity in the group around the fire and the cooking pots also affected us on a deeper level. For thousands of years, our ancestors have shared their microbes by eating out of the same bowls and living physically close to each other. Family, friends and acquaintances must have acted as a collective reservoir for a common, healthy gut flora.

Analyses of fossilised faeces from ancient camp sites indicate that our ancestors' gut flora was similar to that of today's indigenous peoples. And among them, the differences between each individual's gut bacteria are far smaller than in modern society.

We can see the same pattern among primates, where those who often have physical contact with each other also have the most similar gut flora. The group shares an ecosystem of gut microbes that may have given rise to personalities with similar characteristics and dispositions.

Primitive people largely live outdoors and often touch soil and plants, and it's common for children to be reared jointly and moved from one set of adult arms to another. This has made many researchers question whether the nuclear family with its relatively few members is ideal for developing a healthy gut flora.

Cheerful centenarians

We can still see the traditional importance of communal eating in what are called the blue zones – geographically delimited areas where a given individual has the greatest chance of living to the age of 100.

In the last ten years, both Niklas and I have several times visited these places, which are located on the Japanese island of Okinawa, in eastern Sardinia, on the Greek island of Ikaria and the Nicoya Peninsula in Costa Rica.

Research shows that people who live in these blue zones are healthier and more rarely affected by cardiovascular diseases, dementia, diabetes and a number of types of cancer.

The blue zones are a fantastic source of information and a kind of cheat sheet for when new theories on food and health are developed. Anything that's worked for the people who have lived longest and been healthiest can't be completely wrong.

And it's startling how often exactly the kind of varied, fibre-rich and tasty food that people have always eaten in the blue zones is now being highlighted by independent researchers for its positive effect on the gut flora and health.

Of course not everything is down to food, but in the blue zones food constitutes a central part of a lifestyle in which people have also found a healthy balance between physical activity and relaxation and where socialising with family and friends is more important than the hunt for status and gadgets.

People grow their own vegetables and rear animals, and the food they eat isn't merely healthy but really tasty too. It's over meals that often last for hours that people meet, boast about their successes with ingredients and dishes, laugh and talk about everything between heaven and earth.

This is an environment where it's always easy to feel welcome!

On the Japanese island of Okinawa, I once went down to the beach at dawn with 90-year-old Fumiyasu Yamakawa, to join in with the senior exercise session. This turned out to be an hour's quite sweaty workout that ended with ten minutes of yoga headstands.

After this, they all came together and carried out a gentle series of movements inspired by karate and Okinawan dance. Then they suddenly all shouted 'Yahoo!' out at the sea and laughed for all they were worth.

'People who can make a long noise live longest,' explained Fumiyasu Yamakawa later. 'Those who laugh a lot stay healthy.'

He isn't wrong. Laughing is probably good for the lungs and breathing in the same way as choral singing, and seeking out positive emotions seems to have a stress-relieving function.

Whole roasted butternut squash with black kale, kohlrabi and quinoa

Butternut squashes don't only contain good fibre and beta-carotene; the seeds are also full of tryptophan – a precursor of the happiness hormone serotonin. They also contain lots of zinc and magnesium, deficiencies of which can contribute to depression.

1 butternut squash
4–6 black kale leaves
1–2 kohlrabi
100g cooked quinoa
½ bunch of watercress
  (or pea shoots)
100g feta cheese
3 tablespoons pumpkin
  seeds, toasted
2 tablespoons cold-pressed
  rapeseed oil
salt

1. Preheat the oven to 200°C.
2. Halve the butternut squash lengthways and remove the seeds.
3. Place on a baking tray with the cut side down, and bake in the oven for approximately 40 minutes until it is soft in the middle.
4. Boil about two litres of lightly salted water in a wide saucepan.
5. Remove the stems of the black kale. Peel the kohlrabi and cut into 2cm cubes.
6. Place the kohlrabi in the boiling water and allow to boil for 1 minute. Add the black kale and allow to boil for a further 30 seconds. Drain off the water and leave to steam.
7. Cut the butternut squash into 6–8 pieces and mix with the kohlrabi and black kale.
8. Top with quinoa, watercress, feta cheese, toasted pumpkin seeds and rapeseed oil.

Roast chicken breast on the bone with lemon and grilled salad

This flavour combination is incredibly tasty! Can you use any kind of chicken? No, remember that animal protection rules vary considerably between different countries and labels. Organic chickens live a more natural life and grow more slowly. If you can find chicken of a slow-growing breed that's an extra bonus. If you like meat, eat less but of better quality!

1 whole chicken
2 tablespoons salt
2 lemons and/or oranges, cut in half
300ml water
2 bay leaves
2 shallots, chopped
3 tablespoons olive oil
4 little gem lettuces, cut in half
1 bunch of rapeseed stalks

1. Preheat the oven to 230°C.
2. Rub the chicken thoroughly with the salt.
3. Place the chicken and lemon in an ovenproof dish. Place in the oven and roast for 20 minutes.
4. Reduce the temperature to 175°C.
5. Pour the water over the chicken and continue to roast for 30 minutes or until the juices run clear. Baste the chicken with the liquid in the bottom of the tray every 5 minutes.
6. Remove the chicken from the oven and leave to stand for 10 minutes.
7. Pour the juices from the chicken into a saucepan and thoroughly squeeze in the juice from the lemons.
8. Place the bay leaves and shallots into the saucepan with the liquid and allow to boil until it is reduced by half.
9. Remove from the heat and add the olive oil.
10. Grill the lettuce on a high heat for 2-3 minutes (or fry in a hot pan with a little oil).
11. Carve out the chicken breast and serve with the lemon sauce and griddled lettuce.

Note! The idea here is to show how you can use a whole chicken to give three dinners for the week (see the recipe here and on pages 133 and 145).

Beans with tomato sauce, toasted sourdough bread and basil

When you visit the Italian countryside, this is the kind of dish you're sometimes presented by the host. Just in passing, while you wait for the next dish, but secretly fully aware that it will be an immediate success. It is delicious served as an accompaniment to meatballs or grilled pork chops, or just a simple green salad.

3 tablespoons chopped shallots
1 teaspoon chopped garlic
1 teaspoon chopped chilli
3 tablespoons olive oil, plus extra
   for drizzling
1 tablespoon tomato purée
100ml white wine
300g chopped tomatoes
200g tomatoes (cut into
   3cm cubes)
8–10 basil leaves, stalks separated
5 slices of sourdough bread
   (see recipe on page 206)
300g cooked large white beans
100g Parmesan
a pinch of black pepper,
   freshly ground

1. Sauté the shallots, garlic and chilli in the olive oil without allowing them to brown (3–4 minutes).
2. Add the tomato purée and continue to fry for 1–2 minutes.
3. Add the wine and reduce to half the volume.
4. Add the chopped tomatoes, fresh tomatoes and the basil stalks.
5. Simmer for 30 minutes at a low temperature.
6. Preheat the oven to 75°C.
7. Cut off the crusts from the bread and cut the bread into roughly 3cm cubes.
8. Place the bread on a baking tray, drizzle with a little olive oil and toast in the oven until golden brown, around 3–4 minutes – the middle should ideally still be a bit soft.
9. Heat the beans in the tomato sauce, and then add the croutons.
10. Let the croutons soak in the tomato sauce for a few minutes so that they absorb the sauce.
11. Serve with basil leaves, Parmesan and freshly ground black pepper.

HOW DO YOU REALLY EAT?

CHAPTER 9.

Mindful eating

What did you eat this morning? Perhaps you remember that, but what did it look like, and how did it taste and smell? It isn't only what you eat but also how you eat that affects your mood. Brand new research sponsored by the European Commission indicates that people who eat mindfully are less depressed. So focus! Absorb the food with all your senses.

We already know that people who eat mindfully and thoughtfully more easily lose weight, feel more balanced mentally and are more rarely affected by cardiovascular diseases. There are also results indicating that mindfulness in general has a positive impact on depression.

A fascinating new study within the EU's MoodFood project also shows that people who eat mindfully, focus on their sensory impressions and aren't interrupted during their meals run a lower risk of being affected by depression.

'This is the first study to investigate the subject, and we can't yet say how cause and effect work. But having said that, the direct connection was actually even stronger than we'd suspected from the outset,' says researcher Laura Winkens, from Vrije Universiteit in Amsterdam.

This ambitious study included 4,500 people in Denmark, the Netherlands and Spain, and the effect was the same in all three countries.

Why is this? Laura Winkens' hypothesis is that by learning to eat mindfully, we can win on several levels at the same time. Firstly, we avoid sweets, cakes and unhealthy fast food that automatically follows from unconscious eating. It also has the bonus that we become more interested in healthy, varied and well-prepared food.

So what is mindful eating?

Laura Winkens' group has developed a method based on four factors.

Focused eating. Experience tastes and aromas. Use all your senses and take your time. Look at the food, imagine how it feels, tastes, smells or will sound when you chew it. Observe with all of your senses how the food feels in your mouth.

Laura Winkens: 'Take a deep breath before you start eating. Lay your fork down between each bite.'

Explore hunger and satiety.
Eat only when you are hungry. Stop eating when you're full, even if there's food left on the plate. Experiment with going hungry for a while and learn to distinguish between real hunger, temporary cravings and just general restlessness.

Laura Winkens: 'Most people don't know what hunger means. Don't eat simply because you normally do at a certain time. Try drinking a glass of water and see if the feelings of hunger dissipate. Real hunger doesn't do that. Start by putting just a small amount of food on your plate, and then take more if you really need to.'

Mindful eating. Avoid eating automatically. Instead, take a step back and think about whether you really need to eat. Respect the food, the work and lives that have gone into it. Explore your thoughts about food.

Laura Winkens: 'The classic sign of automatic eating is when you're eating a packet of crisps and suddenly they're all gone. Or you take a new bite of something almost before you've swallowed the previous one. One tip is to serve fruit unpeeled and nuts in their shells so that you're forced to slow down.'

Eat without interruptions. Eat at a dining table without looking at your phone or the TV. Don't eat at your desk, in the car or on the way somewhere. Ideally, eat with other people, but in silence, focusing on the food, at least to begin with.

'Of course, eating with other people is very social, and meals where the family come together play an important role. But when it comes to mindful eating, this can also have negative sides that it's useful to be aware of, such as a tendency to copy other people's eating behaviours and the distraction value of conversation. I think it's a good idea to eat together, but make it a habit to eat in silence in the beginning,' says Laura Winkens.

Three of these four factors have shown a strong link to the

risk of depression in all of the countries investigated. However, the factor that involves hunger and satiety was only studied in the Netherlands, where it didn't seem to play a clear role. This astonished the researchers, but Laura Winkens believes the fact the participants were a little older may have affected their appetites.

The next step is to try to find out what it is about mindful eating that has a positive impact on mental well-being, but also to investigate whether there's a causal relationship.

'People who eat mindfully seem to eat fewer calories than others. One explanation can be that they better retain the memory of earlier meals. And mindful eating probably also leads to healthier food choices,' says Laura Winkens.

Try it yourself: Mindfully eat a raisin

A classic exercise in mindful eating is to eat a raisin.

1. Look at the raisin as if this was the first time you've ever seen one. Discover every detail in its shape.

2. Investigate how many colours you can see.

3. Hold the raisin up to the light. Observe all the darker and lighter areas.

4. Close your eyes, and use your sense of touch. Is the raisin soft or hard? Squarish or round?

5. Smell the raisin. Does it awaken any memories?

6. Listen to the raisin! Hold it up to one ear, squeeze it lightly and roll it between your fingers and try to decide how the raisin sounds.

7. Taste the raisin. Allow it to lie on your tongue for a while before you move the raisin around in your mouth with all of your taste buds at full alert.

8. Finally, take a small bite. Explore the effect. Take another small bite.

9. Feel the signal that your body wants to swallow the raisin, but wait a little longer. Reflect on the raisin's long journey, from the farm via land and perhaps air to the shop and then up to the moment it was intended for, on the way down your throat.

10. Swallow the raisin. Feel how it affects your body.

Fact: Resistant starch

Starch is how plants store energy. The only thing that distinguishes it chemically from normal sugar is that the sugar molecules form long chains.

When these chains are a little shorter, they can be snipped off by the body's own enzymes, so that the pieces of sugar are ultimately small enough to be absorbed by the blood. This process begins in the mouth and continues in the small intestine.

The smaller these pieces of sugar are, the more quickly they are absorbed in the body. If we have poor blood sugar regulation and eat a lot of sweet things, we require a lot of insulin – the hormone that makes sure the level is correct – and then the blood sugar may instead fall too much, making us tired and lethargic.

This is what's normally known as the blood sugar blues. The worse your body handles blood sugar, the more your mood is likely to fluctuate. Sometimes rather hyper and sometimes sad and miserable. It's the same effect that makes you tired after eating.

So what's so great about resistant starch? Well, it has such long chains that they aren't broken down at all by our own enzymes in the small intestine. Instead, they become food for the bacteria living in the colon.

Psychobiotic cooking for beginners

Food that both adds and nourishes bacteria with the potential to make you healthy in both body and soul is sometimes, rather complicatedly, called psychobiotic.

You can help add good bacteria by eating kefir, sauerkraut, kimchi or other things with living lactic acid cultures. In many cases, you already have good bacteria in your stomach, but perhaps not many of them. The trick is to send down fibre to help your good bacteria to flourish.

If you succeed in getting one of the five main groups: legumes, whole grains, alliums, leafy green vegetables and cruciferous plants such as broccoli and green cabbage on your plate as often as you can, you satisfy many microbial tastes.

Accompany this with fruit, berries, nuts, seeds, herbs and mushrooms. Add to this food that's rich in colours and aromas, because the substances that produce these effects are those the gut bacteria use to manufacture healthy hormones, signal substances, vitamins, metabolites and other substances the body needs. Include as many colours as possible on your plate.

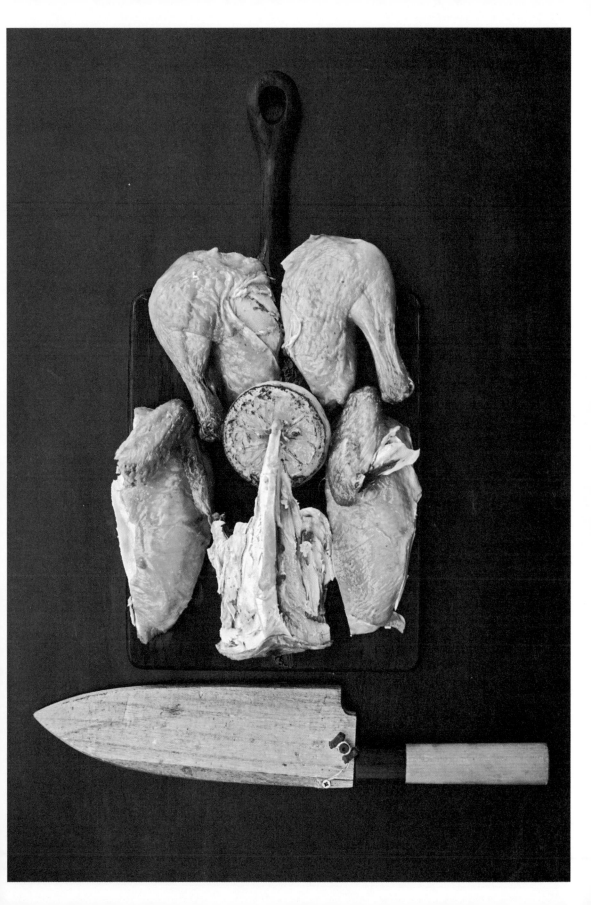

Roast chicken soup with crudités

Soup isn't merely tasty, it's also excellent in terms of sustainability. If we choose to eat meat, it's a ridiculous waste to throw away half of it, so this recipe makes use of the best flavours, which are usually found closest to the bones.

1 whole chicken
2 lemons and/or oranges,
  cut in half
600ml water
2 yellow onions
2 sticks of celery
3 cloves of garlic
3 parsnips
1 bulb of fennel
2 tablespoons butter
200ml white wine
500ml cream
3–4 tablespoons sherry vinegar
3–4 beetroots (red/white/Chioggia)
2 tablespoons olive oil
salt

1. Preheat the oven to 230°C.
2. Rub the chicken thoroughly with 2 tablespoons of salt.
3. Place the chicken and lemon in an ovenproof dish. Roast in the oven for 20 minutes.
4. Reduce the temperature to 175°C.
5. Pour 300ml of the water over the chicken and continue to roast for 30 minutes or until the juices run clear. Baste the chicken with the liquid in the bottom of the tray every 5 minutes.
6. Remove the chicken from the oven and leave to stand for 10 minutes.
7. Cut off the breast meat (see recipe on page 122) and set the wings aside. Cut off the legs (see recipe on page 145).
8. Cut the carcass into 6-8 pieces.
9. Peel and roughly slice the onions, celery, garlic and parsnips.
10. Peel the fennel and roughly chop half. Set the other half aside.
11. Fry the roughly chopped vegetables in the butter in a large saucepan (about 5 litres) until golden brown.
12. Add the chicken carcass and wings, and continue to fry for 3-4 minutes.
13. Add the wine and allow to cook until it has reduced by half.
14. Add the cream and the remaining 300ml of water, bring to the boil and allow to cook for 60 minutes over a low heat.
15. Remove from the heat and leave to stand for 30 minutes.
16. Strain through a sieve and season the soup with 1-2 tablespoons of sherry vinegar and salt.
17. Slice the beetroots and the remaining fennel thinly, ideally with a mandoline. Mix with the olive oil, the remaining sherry vinegar and salt.
18. Serve the salad alongside the soup, topped with the wings.

Whole roast sweet potato with mint, coriander, chilli and cashew nuts

You can't get healthier than this. During my very first visit to Okinawa, I learned that the generation that was the oldest and healthiest on Earth had eaten sweet potatoes every day for most of their lives. So it's no coincidence that this is the crop the UN recommends as first aid during famines. And here we add nutritious beans, olive oil, nuts and coriander.

4 sweet potatoes
½ pointed white cabbage
300g mung beans
1 red chilli
1 bunch of coriander
1 bunch of mint
100g cashew nuts
4 tablespoons olive oil

1. Preheat the oven to 200°C.
2. Scrub the sweet potatoes and rinse with cold water.
3. Place on a baking tray and roast in the oven for about 40 minutes. Test them with a skewer – they should be soft in the centre but still with some bite.
4. Bring a large pan of salted water to the boil. Cook the cabbage leaves for 1 minute. Cool in cold water.
5. Blanch the mung beans for 10 seconds in salted water. Cool in cold water.
6. Thinly slice the chilli.
7. Pick the leaves off the coriander and mint.
8. Coarsely chop the cashew nuts.
9. Remove the potatoes from the oven.
10. Warm the cabbage and beans with a few tablespoons of water in a saucepan.
11. Serve the sweet potatoes with the skin on, with the cabbage and mung beans. Top with the cashew nuts, chilli, mint and coriander leaves and drizzle the oil over.

Whole grilled zander with garlic cream and potato salad

We feel good when we eat fish several times a week – so make a nice dish of it! And what's more delicious than a freshly caught zander? If the potato salad is served cold, some resistant starch re-forms. This means that your blood sugar won't increase so much from the boiled potatoes.

1 bunch of haricots verts
500g cold boiled potatoes
2 tablespoons capers
1 tablespoon chopped dill
1 whole zander or perch, 1–1½kg, gutted and scaled
lemon wedges for serving
salt

Garlic cream
3 tablespoons water
2 tablespoons French mustard
2 egg yolks
1 tablespoon lemon juice
2 cloves of garlic
200ml olive oil

1. Bring a large pan of salted water to the boil. Cook the haricots verts for 20 seconds. Cool in cold water. Leave in a sieve to drain.
2. Preheat the oven or grill to 175°C.
3. Cut the potatoes into 3cm cubes.
4. Whisk together the water, mustard, egg yolks and lemon juice. Grate the garlic and add it.
5. Continue to whisk and add the olive oil in an even flow until you achieve a garlic cream with a smooth consistency. If it gets too thick, add a few spoonfuls of water.
6. Mix the potatoes, beans, capers, dill and a few spoonfuls of garlic cream. Season with more garlic if desired.
7. Rub the fish with plenty of salt.
8. Grill or oven bake the fish for 20–40 minutes depending on the size of the fish. The internal temperature must be about 48°C.
9. Serve with lemon wedges, potato salad and extra garlic cream.

FLAVOURS FOR BOTH BIG AND SMALL

CHAPTER 10.

Niklas: How I got my children to eat (almost) anything

The idea of a pleasant meal can seem simple, but as any parent knows, it doesn't happen automatically. There are many pitfalls along the way and it's ultimately all about prioritising. Due to a lack of time, I've sometimes applied simple solutions, but this is short-term thinking. In the longer term – over an entire childhood – you're guaranteed to save time as a parent if your children develop a positive relationship with eating and cooking at an early age.

Niklas has experienced the same problems as everyone else. Sometimes it makes no difference if you're a Michelin-starred chef. At the dining table at home, it was still Niklas' children who took command and complained bitterly if they didn't get frozen ready-made meatballs, or turned up their noses at the main course and refused to eat anything but bread.

But who was it that decreed children should only enjoy pancakes, meatballs and macaroni or spaghetti bolognese? Here are a few of Niklas' hard learned lessons.

Introduce new flavours at an early age, ideally from five months and onwards. Children have an innate love of sweet things, and also enjoy salt, fat and umami. There's a window up to the age of two when children will also accept tart and bitter food.

Then they start displaying what's known as neophobia. This means that children avoid bitter flavours, probably because these flavours have been linked to poisons and danger for thousands of years. Today we know that many bitter herbs are actually edible, and in fact particularly nutritious.

'If you allow your children to taste bitter foods at an early age, they'll already be used to the flavour and will accept it and enjoy it later too,' says Niklas.

'Otherwise it can take up to 15 tastings before the child is accustomed to the new flavour. That may not sound like much, but it's guaranteed to feel like a lot more...'

Small children like eating each thing separately. Think one colour and one structure per bowl, and avoid green dots of chopped herbs. This makes the child suspicious. Asian food is particularly useful, according to Niklas. It's easy to add new flavours. Example: fried noodles with sweetcorn and chicken.

Don't think 'kids' food'. French children are known for eating everything. So what's the secret? Well, kids' food is an almost unknown concept in France. Instead, the children get the same food as the adults, and schools usually serve a four course lunch. Anyone who doesn't like it has to go hungry, but because they're all used to eating like this, very little is wasted.

Create stories about the food. When Niklas and Katarina's children were first served quinoa, their parents told them that it came from the Inca people. That sounded exciting and gave it a context. Does the recipe come from a relative? Call it 'Granny's saffron cake' or 'Uncle Pete's curry'.

Dare to exploit sugar. For good reasons, sugar is a red flag to many people, and the majority of us eat far too much of it. Repetitive sweetness disrupts children's taste development and has no medical benefits. But if sugar is used as a creative spice in small doses, it reinforces the other flavours and can change the texture of the food, making it more palatable.

If a little sugar can help a child to eat fibre-rich vegetables that aren't normally popular, the benefit is much greater than the risk. The point is that it's you as the parent who takes command.

Niklas usually stir fries the kind of vegetables his children don't like eating, such as haricots verts, with palm sugar or maple syrup. If one component tastes sweet, the salty flavour of something else is emphasised. Even ketchup in moderate amounts can be a way to get the child to more easily eat a nutritious food. Why not make your own?

Eat with your children. Don't believe that your children will always do as you say, but they will probably gradually do as you do.

One parental trap it's easy to fall into is to eat the same tasteless macaroni and sausage as they do 'because it's easier'. Another is that the children eat on their own.

One way to counteract these short-sighted shortcuts is to cook food where you can vary the content so that the meals are also suitable for adults. Make an extra topping mixture, for example. Pizza, tacos or baked potatoes are unwritten sheets that can be filled with different contents, while the children think you're all eating the same thing.

141

Pasta al dente with sage, butter and pine nuts

Pasta tastes great, but won't it make me fat? No, because moderation and quality are the keywords. The GI value is lower if you choose pasta made from durum wheat and serve it al dente. As always, you have to see the meal as a whole. Here we balance the pasta with black pepper and pine nuts that stabilise the blood sugar and feelings of hunger.

400g pappardelle, dried
2 cloves of garlic
3 tablespoons butter
8–10 sage leaves, plus extra
   to garnish
50g Parmesan
3 tablespoons pine nuts, toasted
black pepper for serving

1. Cook the pasta al dente, according to the instructions on the packaging. Drain and leave to steam thoroughly.
2. Thinly slice the garlic.
3. Brown the butter slightly and add the sage and garlic.
4. Add the pasta and mix thoroughly.
5. Serve with Parmesan shavings, toasted pine nuts, extra finely sliced sage and freshly ground black pepper.

Roast chicken legs with spelt, tomato and herbs

A dish inspired by South American chimichurri, a tasty sauce that also works very well as a marinade. There are contradictory theories about where and how this sauce came about, but its roots can be found in Argentina and Uruguay, from where it spread to Mexico and the rest of the world.

1 whole chicken
2 lemons and/or oranges,
    cut in half
300ml water
1 red onion
3 cloves of garlic
1 red chilli
2 tablespoons olive oil
4–6 tomatoes
200g cooked whole spelt
1 bag of fresh leaf spinach
1 bunch of parsley
1 bunch of oregano
1 sprig of thyme
1–2 tablespoons sherry vinegar
salt

1. Preheat the oven to 230°C.
2. Rub the chicken thoroughly with 2 tablespoons of salt.
3. Place the chicken and lemon in an ovenproof dish. Roast in the oven for 20 minutes.
4. Reduce the temperature to 175°C.
5. Pour the water over the chicken and continue to roast for 30 minutes or until the juices run clear. Baste the chicken with the liquid in the bottom of the tray every 5 minutes.
6. Remove the chicken from the oven and leave to stand for 10 minutes.
7. Cut off the breast meat (see recipe on page 122) and set the wings aside (see recipe on page 133).
8. Cut off the legs and set the carcass aside (see recipe on page 133).
9. Peel the red onion and garlic and slice thinly. Slice the chilli.
10. Fry the onion, garlic and chilli for 1–2 minutes in olive oil.
11. Cut the tomatoes into roughly 3cm cubes and fry with the onion and garlic for a few minutes.
12. Add the cooked spelt and mix until it's warmed through. Stir in the spinach and herbs.
13. Season with sherry vinegar and salt.
14. Serve the spelt with the roast chicken legs.

Bean burgers with caraway and garlic

There are lots of good bean burgers. Here's a tasty version that can be served as an alternative to hamburgers or with salad leaves and aioli as an accompaniment. Rich in both protein and fibre.

400g cooked kidney beans
400g cooked black beans
1 teaspoon salt
2 pinches of black pepper,
    freshly ground
a pinch of ground caraway
2 cloves of garlic, peeled
1 yellow onion, peeled and
    roughly sliced
1 tablespoon olive oil
2–3 tablespoons potato flour
oil for frying

1. Drain the beans thoroughly.
2. Blend the spices, garlic, onion and olive oil into a smooth paste.
3. Add the beans and blend briefly – the beans should still be chunky.
4. Add the potato flour so that you can shape the burgers. If necessary, add a few more beans.
5. Shape the burgers – you should get 8 small ones or 4 big ones – and fry in oil until golden brown on both sides.

Overnight oats with lingonberries and milk

Mix your porridge the night before and place the bowl in the fridge ... and hey presto! – the next day, the breakfast is ready to serve.

2 tablespoons linseeds
3 tablespoons sunflower seeds
2 tablespoons walnuts,
   coarsely chopped
200g oat flakes
600ml milk (or oat milk
   or almond milk)
2 tablespoons honey
1 teaspoon salt
3 tablespoons lingonberries
   (fresh or frozen)

1. Preheat the oven to 175°C.
2. Toast the linseeds and sunflower seeds in the oven for about 10 minutes, stirring very regularly so they don't burn.
3. Remove and leave to cool.
4. Mix with the walnuts and oats.
5. Add 400ml of milk and place in the fridge overnight.
6. In the morning, stir and add more milk if required to get the right consistency.
7. Season with honey and salt.
8. Top with lingonberries and milk. Serve with more honey, if liked. We've garnished ours with sorrel, and you can also garnish it with lingon flowers.

EMOTIONAL UPSETS

CHAPTER II.

Violence and vitamins

The food on your plate helps you to control your impulses. Researchers have long argued about whether sugar can cause hyper-activity. The results are contradictory. But it's when we look at diets as a whole that the link becomes clearer. And few people have such poor eating habits as convicted violent criminals.

Massive Geir breaks an egg with his fingertips and stirs the frying pan with a spatula that almost disappears in his enormous hand.

On this day in 2009, I found myself in the national prison in the city of Bergen – a closed prison where 157 of Norway's worst criminals had been sent after being sentenced for theft or violent crime.

'When people come here they're skinny, but after just a few years they've gained 50 kilos. There are biscuits and waffles the whole time, and we need to get sugar out of the desserts,' said Geir, when we stood in the kitchenette outside his cell. He had been a vegetarian since two years previously and was very careful about what he ate.

The sweets and cakes that many of the other inmates regularly bought from the prison kiosk weren't merely contributing to obesity. Pioneering research, including in this prison in Bergen, had shown that junk food reduces violent criminals' impulse control and increases the risk of conflict and violence.

A survey within the Norwegian prison service had already shown that 85% of all inmates had some form of diagnosis or mental problem. But the controversial question was whether poor eating habits could contribute to criminality.

'When we started to investigate how much nutrition the prisoners got, we realised they had very low levels of Omega-3 fatty acids from fish in their blood,' explained the prison's former chef, Lena Backe, who was showing me around the prison. She was now studying nutritional science at the University of Bergen.

Continued analyses showed that it wasn't only healthy fish fats that were missing from the prison diet. Blood tests revealed that many prisoners also had very low levels of vitamins D, C and B6, folate and thiamine, and of the minerals selenium, zinc and iron.

In an experiment, 25 of the 157 prisoners were given a diet where fish containing Omega-3 fatty acids was on the menu three days a week. A control group of 25 other inmates was given the standard menu with fish once a week.

The results confirmed the suspicion – there seemed to be a link between diet and the prisoners' cognitive abilities and emotional regulation.

This wasn't surprising. The same thing had already been shown in a prestudy among 57 of the prisoners. It turned out that just like physical exercise, a diet containing a lot of fish positively affected the prisoners' impulse control, while sugar had a negative impact.

Are you one of those people who sometimes get cross and blame it on low blood sugar levels if you miss breakfast? Well imagine the mood swings in somebody who for several weeks has lived on just cigarettes, overly sweet coffee, hotdogs and lots of beer. That's a normal diet

for many criminals, according to the study. 'We know that 85% of all violent crimes are impulsive actions that are planned for less than 15 minutes, and we also know that poor food impairs impulse control,' explained a regional manager within the Norwegian prison service.

'If we can reduce the number of violent crimes, even by just a few percent, by serving good food, that's a great deal gained for a minimal cost. Many violent criminals have extremely poor eating habits. This means that the potential for improving nutrient intake is extremely large in this particular group,' he continued.

While criminologists have shown a limited interest in studying the importance of diet, the military has been more open to innovations, not least in Norway.

The Norwegian Navy has investigated how food can help a sniper to act correctly in extremely stressful situations while under fire.

The answer turned out to be linked to the heart's ability to quickly change the rhythm of the pulse. Does your heart thump in your chest if you get nervous or have done something stupid? That's a good sign, which increases your ability to handle stress and also contributes to being able to feel regret.

But your pulse also needs to be able to quickly adapt downwards again. In many violent criminals, their pulse never increases when they do something wrong. Perhaps this is what is meant by doing something 'in cold blood'.

The heart's ability to quickly change rhythm is known as heart rate variability (HRV). Results have shown that HRV is a more certain factor than both social background and previous criminality in predicting whether someone will commit a new violent crime. People who are extremely aggressive often have a low HRV.

A flexible heart that quickly changes rhythm can effectively supply the brain and body with the extra strength it needs to deal with unexpected events and emotions. The cognitive abilities are reinforced, which means that it is easier even in stressful situations to reason about problems, plan and make considered decisions.

It has been shown that both physical exercise and a varied diet with sufficient quantities of Omega-3 fats from oily fish have a positive impact on heart rate variability.

In the early 2000s in the UK, Oxford researcher Bernard Gesch carried out a study at the high security prison for violent young offenders in Aylesbury, which is renowned for serious disciplinary problems.

Three out of four prisoners had low or very low intakes of zinc, selenium, iodine, magnesium and potassium – and intakes of salt which were far too high.

Bernard Gesch moved into one of the prison's solitary confinement cells, which was converted into a combined office and clinic. Over nine months, he then studied 231 young criminals, of which half were given supplements containing 28 vitamins, minerals and fatty acids in levels corresponding to the recommended daily doses.

'We saw a rapid and significant reduction in the number of violent incidents. The reduction was between 25 and 37% depending on what we measured,' said Bernard Gesch when I interviewed him.

When the trial ended, violence rose quickly to the previous level, and the researcher's clinic was turned back into a solitary confinement cell.

Bernard Gesch was careful to emphasise that he didn't believe Omega-3 fatty acids in fish, or other individual supplements, were the entire explanation of the effect. Instead he looked at the diet as a whole and pointed out that body and brain need a large number of vitamins and minerals to function correctly.

According to Gesch it isn't just coincidence that many violent crimes are committed by young men in the late teenage years as no other group has such an extensive need for ample, varied food.

The brain is a power station that represents 2% of our mass but uses 20% of the body's energy. The brain's needs are greatest in the later teenage years during the final development of important brain functions. But in boys this coincides with a significant increase in muscle mass. And this is often a chain reaction because late teenage boys often have poor eating habits.

The result is poor impulse control, mental problems and a tendency to resort to violence and aggression in stressful situations.

'In the last 50 years we have seen enormous changes in the food we eat, and researchers started studying how it affected mortality in cases of heart disease. It's only in recent years that we've begun to realise that something that can damage the heart can naturally also affect the brain, which is a much more sensitive organ. Today we're starting to understand that when we change our diet, it radically affects our brains,' said Gesch.

Since the Aylesbury study, researchers in the USA and the Netherlands have produced similar results. But thus far there is no research that goes one step further and investigates whether, and if so how, impulse control – alongside other conceivable factors such as social structures, vulnerability and drugs – can be linked to our microbes. Because imagine if some bacteria can make us more prone to violence than others!

I have interviewed top researchers who say that this could trigger a penal revolution. If some junk food is shown to nourish bacteria that contribute to violent behaviour, defence lawyers would be able to argue that the food industry bears responsibility for their clients' criminality.

- - - - - - - - - - - - - - - - - - - -

A British car thief's diet

Breakfast: nothing.
Lunch: 4.5 cups of coffee with 2½ heaped teaspoons of sugar in each.
Afternoon: 3–5 cups of coffee with 2½ heaped teaspoons of sugar in each.
Dinner: Chips, egg, 2 slices of white bread, ketchup. 5 cups of tea or coffee with 2½ heaped teaspoons of sugar in each.
Evening: 5 cups of tea or coffee with 2½ heaped teaspoons of sugar in each. 3–4 beers.
Miscellaneous: 20 cigarettes. About £2 worth of sweets and biscuits.

Source: Gesch et al. *Br J Psychiatry*. 2002.

- - - - - - - - - - - - - - - - - - - -

Blood orange and Brussels sprout salad

Blood oranges and other citrus fruit have been around for so long that we almost take them for granted. Here they balance the flavour of the Brussels sprouts, but all citrus fruit also increase the uptake of minerals from seeds and nuts.

500g Brussels sprouts
1 blood orange (or orange/
   grapefruit/pomelo)
2 tablespoons olive oil
2 tablespoons chopped shallots
100g walnuts, roasted

1. Remove any damaged leaves from the Brussels sprouts. Cut into halves.
2. Grate the zest of the blood orange.
3. Peel the orange with a sharp knife, cut out the segments and squeeze the juice from the remaining membranes.
4. Warm a frying pan over a high heat and fry the Brussels sprouts in olive oil.
5. When the Brussels sprouts have browned, add the shallots, orange zest and juice. Allow the juice to reduce.
6. Serve with orange segments and top with coarsely chopped walnuts.

Kalops with beetroot and sauerkraut salad

Kalops, a traditional Scandinavian dish, has been cooked in Sweden and Finland for hundreds of years and is found in a classic Swedish cookery book dating back to the 1700s. This is a slightly richer version with carrots and the addition of a little beer. One tip is not to skimp on the cooking time, so that the meat becomes really tender.

1kg braising steak
1 tablespoon butter
2 carrots
2 yellow onions
2 tablespoons wheat flour
500ml veal stock
500ml beer (lager or ale)
3 bay leaves
12 allspice berries
2–4 beetroots
1 apple
200g sauerkraut
1 teaspoon whole cumin
1 bunch of parsley, for serving
salt

1. Cut the meat into 5cm cubes.
2. Fry the meat in butter in a large pan until lightly browned.
3. Peel the carrots and onions. Cut into large pieces and fry with the meat for 2–3 minutes.
4. Add the flour and continue to fry for a few minutes.
5. Add the stock and beer, a little at a time while stirring continuously. Bring to the boil.
6. Add the bay leaves and allspice berries.
7. Leave to cook for 1½ hours over a low heat or until the meat is tender.
8. Shred the beetroots and apple. Mix with the sauerkraut and cumin.
9. Season the stew with salt to taste and top with parsley.
10. Serve with the beetroot and sauerkraut salad.

Sauerkraut and duck

Once upon a time, people consumed far more living bacteria cultures than we do today, via fermented food. Like sauerkraut. Try to consume at least some lactic acid bacteria every day. It also tastes great.

1 yellow onion, chopped
2 tablespoons duck fat or butter
500g sauerkraut
1 teaspoon whole cumin
2 bay leaves
1 apple, peeled and grated
2 tablespoons apple cider vinegar
200ml chicken stock
200ml dry white wine
1 bunch of thyme
2 duck breasts
French mustard for serving
salt

1. Fry the onion in duck fat (or butter) over a high heat in a large saucepan.
2. When the onion starts to brown, add the sauerkraut and continue to fry for a few minutes.
3. Add the cumin, bay leaves, grated apple, vinegar, stock, wine and thyme.
4. Reduce the heat and allow to simmer over low heat for 45 minutes. Season with salt.
5. Remove any sinew from the duck breasts.
6. Make a criss-cross pattern of fine, closely spaced incisions in the duck skin and sprinkle with salt.
7. Preheat the oven to 175°C.
8. Place the duck breasts in a cold frying pan with the skin side downwards.
9. Place the pan over a high heat.
10. Fry until the skin is golden brown, then turn the breasts over and continue to fry (1 minute).
11. Remove the duck breast from the pan and place in an ovenproof dish.
12. Place in the oven for about 10 minutes (until you obtain an internal temperature of 56°C).
13. Remove from the oven and leave to stand for 6-8 minutes.
14. Slice the duck and serve with the sauerkraut and French mustard. This is great with roast potatoes.

Venison stew with 'Nordic tabbouleh' and lingonberries

One idea with the new Nordic cuisine is to be open to influences from outside while keeping our boots firmly anchored in the Nordic forests. Like in this venison stew with a Nordic version of the parsley salad so often served in the Middle East.

1kg venison or other game
  stewing meat
2 yellow onions, peeled
2 tablespoons butter
8 juniper berries
3 bay leaves
5 sprigs of thyme
6 black peppercorns
400ml red wine
400ml game stock or veal stock
4 carrots
1 celeriac (approx. half
  the quantity of carrots)
salt

'Nordic tabbouleh'
100g quinoa
¼ white cabbage
1 teaspoon salt
2 bunches of parsley
  or edible weeds
3 tablespoons frozen lingonberries
3 tablespoons cold-pressed
  rapeseed oil

1. Cut the meat and onions into roughly 4cm cubes.
2. Fry the meat and onions in butter over a high heat in a large saucepan until lightly browned.
3. Add the herbs and spices, wine and stock.
4. Cook the meat until tender over a low heat – approx. 1½ hours.
5. Peel the carrots and celery. Cut into roughly 3cm cubes and add to the stew after 1 hour.
6. Season with salt.
7. Cook the quinoa according to the packaging and cool.
8. Slice the white cabbage thinly and mix with 1 teaspoon of salt. Knead for 2 minutes so that the white cabbage softens.
9. Roughly chop the parsley leaves/weeds.
10. Mix the quinoa, white cabbage, parsley, lingonberries and rapeseed oil into a version of Nordic tabbouleh and serve with the stew.

Grass-fed beef with barley, herbs and carrot salad

As we all know, cows have stomachs that are ideal for ruminating grass. They do this so well that they obtain lots of protein and good fats from something we wouldn't get anything from at all. The problem for both cows and humans arises when they are instead served feed based on seeds. This gives the cows stomach ache. And we waste a lot of resources. Because we can eat seeds ourselves.

100g whole barley
8–12 heritage carrots
2 tablespoons spirit vinegar, 12%
500–800g beef sirloin (4 slices)
1 tablespoon oil for frying
4 tablespoons butter
1 bunch of herbs (e.g. thyme,
  sage, rosemary)
salt

1. Cook the barley according to the instructions on the packaging.
2. Slice the carrots thinly on a mandoline.
3. Mix the carrots with a few pinches of salt and the spirit vinegar.
4. Set the carrots aside at room temperature.
5. Salt the beef on both sides.
6. Fry on both sides in a frying pan with a little oil until lightly browned.
7. Add butter and a couple of sprigs of thyme or other herbs. Baste the meat with the warm butter and continue to fry for 2–3 minutes on both sides until medium rare (internal temperature 48°C).
8. Combine the barley, carrots and remaining herbs. Season with a couple of spoonfuls of butter from the meat and serve with the meat.

WE'RE ALL
DIFFERENT

CHAPTER 12.

Pizza – nutritious for everyone

Whether food is healthy or not doesn't just depend on the food. Different people can react in completely different ways to exactly the same food.

A couple of years ago, an Israeli study was published that acted as a real starting point for what's called personal nutrition. Researchers in Tel Aviv had served 50,000 meals to 900 people and then taken 1.5 million blood samples and you don't want to know how many samples of faeces.

But why? Well, it turned out that the blood sugar spikes after a meal varied significantly from one person to another. A majority of the test people had stable blood sugar from eating a Mediterranean diet, and for most of them their blood sugar increased as expected when they ate pizza, but some people didn't react at all. Several of them had a better reaction to rice than ice cream, but in some cases the reverse was true. The researchers had sourdough bread made from ancient types of grain, but some of the test subjects had better values

from eating processed white bread. Blood sugar levels for some people increased significantly when they ate tomatoes, which are normally considered to be healthy... And so on.

The cause could be found in the participants' gut flora. Although the study doesn't tell us anything about the long-term consequences of absorbing too few vitamins and minerals, the conclusion is still that gut flora combined with our inherited predispositions gives us completely different characteristics when it comes to the food we can eat.

According to the researchers at the Weizmann Institute in Tel Aviv, it's still sensible to give the general advice to eat something like the Mediterranean diet. But their study shows that dietary advice will very soon be significantly more individual.

Of course, the effect of food on the blood sugar is only one of several factors that must be taken into account, but it's probably an important one given the global epidemic of Type 2 diabetes. The next step is to develop personal advice that also takes into account your need for vitamins, minerals and other nutrients.

A pattern that has already begun to crystallise is that healthy food is best for people who are already healthy and have a balanced gut flora. In other words, those who are already rich get richer more easily. That seems unfair, doesn't it?

The advantage is that if we are aware of inequalities, researchers can develop strategies that help everyone and not just those who are already in the best position.

The same thing seems to apply to exercise – it's positive for a healthy gut flora but actually dangerous for an unbalanced stomach.

So in the future will we be able to implant bacteria in our own guts that mean we can better tolerate pizza and ice cream? Yes, probably. But we aren't there yet, and before that we will be able to find out if, as individuals, we belong to the group that can handle a little more without having to have such a bad conscience.

The positive thing is that it seems possible most people can improve the long-term balance in their own gut flora with the help of food. But you have to count on it taking a little while – anywhere from three months to one year.

Microbial detox

The gut bacteria we carry around with us can determine how strongly we react to both beneficial substances and dangerous chemicals.

In many cases, healthy bioactive substances in fruit and vegetables need to encounter the right gut bacteria for us to be able to absorb them into our bodies and benefit from the positive effect.

At the same time, toxic substances can be neutralised by the gut bacteria. One example is the endocrine disruptor bisphenol, which is found in plastics. But the same thing seems to apply to a range of environmental toxins, mycotoxins and even those carcinogenic substances that form when we grill food too much.

The conclusion is that we have an individual sensitivity for many substances. Diversity in the gut is your best defence and researchers hope that in the future they will be able to give us more individually tailored and goal-oriented help to fill the gaps in our own gut flora.

Lentil and game bolognese with white cabbage noodles

Is game more nutritious than other meat from four-legged animals? The question hasn't yet been studied. But wild animals have at least been able to root around in the forest and marinade themselves with a range of herbs. This recipe is a sign of the times: meat is no longer the only main attraction, and there are many alternatives to normal pasta.

300g game mince
2 tablespoons olive oil
1 onion
3 cloves of garlic
3 carrots
2 bay leaves
100g red lentils
200ml red wine
400g chopped tomatoes
200ml water
¼ white cabbage
2 litres boiling water
2 tablespoons apple cider vinegar
100g Parmesan, grated
6–8 fresh oregano leaves
salt and black pepper,
   freshly ground

1. Fry the meat in the olive oil over a medium-high heat for 3–4 minutes.
2. Peel the onion, garlic and carrots. Coarsely grate or grind in a meat grinder.
3. Add the vegetables and bay leaves to the meat and continue to fry for 3–4 minutes.
4. Add the lentils, wine, chopped tomatoes, a pinch of black pepper and the 200ml of water.
5. Leave to simmer until you obtain a thick consistency (about 45 minutes). Add more water if required.
6. Slice the white cabbage thinly and place in a sieve.
7. Pour the boiling water over the cabbage then leave to drain and cool.
8. Squeeze out the liquid and season with 1 teaspoon of salt and the vinegar.
9. Season the stew with salt and serve with the cabbage, grated Parmesan and fresh oregano.

Chard with garlic butter and hazelnuts

Chard was one of the first plants considered as an option to be grown on long journeys in space, for example to Mars. And this wasn't by chance. The dark green leaves and the deep red colour of the stalks indicate high levels of vitamins such as A, C and B6, and not least magnesium, which is often in short supply in people with depression. Chard is also extremely rich in antioxidants.

2–3 bunches of chard
3 tablespoons butter
1 tablespoon grated garlic
8–12 yellow cocktail or cherry
   tomatoes, halved
3 tablespoons hazelnuts, toasted
salt

1. Wash and pick over the chard. Shred thinly.
2. Melt the butter and add the garlic, then immediately remove from the heat so it does not burn.
3. Bring a large pan of lightly salted water to the boil. Cook the chard for 20–30 seconds.
4. Remove the chard, leave to steam thoroughly and place on a dish.
5. Mix the chard and tomatoes with the garlic butter and top with grated or chopped hazelnuts.

Golden beet and kale salad with yoghurt and sunflower seed vinaigrette

Kale is nature's answer to a multivitamin tablet. But yes, the flavour can be a little institutional. Fortunately, the flavour depends on the composition of the meal, which here involves golden beet, yoghurt and a little honey.

2–6 yellow beetroot
200g kale
3 tablespoons sunflower seeds
1 tablespoon cold-pressed
  rapeseed oil
2 teaspoons apple cider vinegar
100ml yoghurt
1–2 tablespoons honey
hazelnuts, roasted

1. Cook the beets in lightly salted water until they are soft.
2. Remove from the heat and leave to cool in the liquid. Peel them when they are still warm – this makes it easier to remove the skin.
3. Remove the kale leaves from the stems and cook for 20-30 seconds in lightly salted boiling water.
4. Remove the kale from the liquid and cool in iced water. Squeeze out the liquid.
5. Cut the peeled beets into small pieces, about 3-4cm, and mix with the kale.
6. Fry the sunflower seeds until golden brown in the rapeseed oil over a medium-high heat (remember that they keep cooking for a little while once off the heat, so remove from the heat just before they are ready or they will burn).
7. Season the sunflower seeds with vinegar.
8. Top the golden beet and kale salad with yoghurt, honey, sunflower seed vinaigrette and crushed roasted hazelnuts.

Apple and white cabbage salad with mint and green peas

'An apple a day keeps the doctor away' runs an old saying which is said to have come from Wales. Apples are full of fibre and antioxidants and a study was recently released that showed people who eat apples visit the doctor less often than others. Many of the bioactive substances are found in the colour, and this can come from the apple encountering the rays of the sun as it grows on the tree. So choose the apple that has done the most sunbathing!

½ white cabbage
3 teaspoons salt
2 tablespoons raisins
3 tablespoons apple cider vinegar
2 tablespoons chopped dill
1 tablespoon chopped mint
2 tablespoons olive oil
100g green peas, cooked
1 apple
3 tablespoons hazelnuts, toasted

1. Thinly slice the white cabbage.
2. Mix with the salt in a large bowl and knead the cabbage for 2-3 minutes until it softens. Drain away any excess water.
3. Mix the cabbage with the raisins, vinegar, dill, mint, olive oil and green peas.
4. Thinly slice the apples over the cabbage salad.
5. Chop the hazelnuts and sprinkle over.

A NORDIC BREEZE

IS BLOWING

Food for Vikings

More than 1,000 years ago, the allegedly superstrong Vikings were ravaging the ancient world, and today Scandinavians are among the most long-lived people in the world. And the Danes are the happiest. There are undoubtedly many explanations for this, but research indicates that dietary habits play a central role in our health. In our previous book, *Happy Food*, we talked about the research that shows we feel good when we eat a Mediterranean diet. Now it's time to take a closer look at Scandinavian food.

In recent years, the Nordic diet has become known all around the world. It's based on ingredients that for hundreds of years were eaten in Sweden, Norway, Denmark, Finland and Iceland.

The main foods are leafy green vegetables, legumes, cabbages and alliums, whole rye grain, barley, oats and wheat, fish, fruits such as apples, pears and even peaches grown in Denmark and southern Sweden, together with berries such as lingonberries and blueberries. In other words, fresh seasonal ingredients that are sustainable and locally grown in the Nordic climate.

I'm sure you're beginning to recognise the pattern. The similarities with *Happy Food* and the Mediterranean diet are striking.

In the centre of the food pyramid on page 180 – the things we should eat a moderate amount of – we find root vegetables, bread, eggs and dairy products, and perhaps a little meat from freely grazing animals, ideally from game.

At the top of the pyramid are the things it's best to eat only a little of, or perhaps not at all, such as processed meats and pastries.

Another difference between the Mediterranean and Nordic diets is that the olive oil is also replaced by rapeseed oil.

Niklas and I think the researchers should also take greater account in their studies of fermented foods such as buttermilk, Icelandic skyr and sauerkraut. These also have a long history in the Scandinavian countries. And we shouldn't forget delicacies such as Swedish *surströmming*, Icelandic *súr hvalur* or Norwegian *rakfisk*, all of which can make both your sense of smell and your taste buds turn somersaults.

The inclusion of fermented foods characterises what's known as the New Nordic Diet, which was first developed by top chefs in Denmark, but soon came to characterise the whole of Nordic gastronomy. The idea is to build further on locally grown ingredients and traditional methods by combining ingredients in new ways and being open to external influences.

Like the Mediterranean diet, the Nordic diet has been linked to a reduced risk of cardiovascular disease and Type 2 diabetes, but also to weight reduction, and a recent comparison showed that the Nordic diet was the one that most reduced the risk of cognitive impairment among the elderly.

Bitter but healthy

Older Nordic types of cabbage and root vegetables with their original tart and bitter flavours are healthier than those we buy in the shops. When researchers in the Danish city of Aarhus grew bitter vegetables that were served to Type 2 diabetics, their conditions very soon improved.

For wine lovers, the concept of *terroir* is well known. It represents the impact of the soil, climate, terrain and tradition on the final product. Flavourful wines are often made from ancient vines that grow in rather barren places where the grapes must struggle to survive. This results in smaller but better harvests with flavourful grapes filled with bioactive substances.

So the question is, is there a *terroir* for vegetables?

A few years ago, researchers at Aarhus University started an exciting project. They looked in the Nordic Gene Bank, where older seeds are preserved, for types of cabbage and root vegetables grown by earlier generations and which have a more bitter flavour than we are used to today. Soon they started growing white cabbage, green cabbage, pointed white cabbage, beetroot, carrots and celeriac.

'For 100 years, cultivation has aimed at reducing the bitter flavours and emphasising sweetness. We soon realised that the older types of vegetables have a much greater flavour variation and that many have strong and quite often bitter flavours,' says researcher Hanne Lakkenborg Kristensen, who leads the project.

Then it was time for the experiment. For two years in a row, bitter cabbage and root vegetables were supplied to a hospital where 45 patients a year were selected and divided into three groups. For 12 weeks, one group was served normal food and a second group was given a special menu with 500 grams per day of vegetables purchased in a shop. The final group was given the same quantity of vegetables but this time the bitter varieties.

'Both years, the effects on the patients' health was very good in the groups that ate a lot of vegetables, but clearly best in the group served the bitter types,' says Hanne Lakkenborg Kristensen.

Samples showed that the patients had improved blood lipid levels and more balanced blood sugar. Some patients with moderate Type 2 diabetes could essentially be declared healthy.

Hanne Lakkenborg Kristensen and the other researchers believe that one explanation is that the flavours come from bioactive substances called glucosinolates, which have a demonstrated positive effect on the blood sugar balance.

We have previously said that the biggest problem with processed Western food is that it's lacking in fibre. But there's another major problem: while the minerals and vitamins are to some extent still intact, the food has also been depleted of bioactive substances.

Hanne Lakkenborg Kristensen has a theory that the rather harsh Nordic climate may have contributed to the development in the region of particularly healthy types of root vegetables which are rich in bioactive substances. In the spring, there is essentially nothing to harvest and for a long time

people have thus had to rely on root vegetables stored over the winter. The types that best coped with being stored are those that contain the most antioxidants and bioactive substances. And they taste ... yes, bitter.

One unexpected side effect is that strong flavours also seem to be more filling.

Now the project, which was initially called MaxVeg, has been expanded and in the follow-up project Bitter-Sund, bitter variants of cauliflower, red cabbage, Savoy cabbage, Brussels sprouts, Hamburg parsley and parsnip are being cultivated. All are organic and are being grown in test plots in a number of different places.

'Several factors play a role, such as the type, soil and climate, but there's a tendency for organically cultivated vegetables to contain more bioactive substances. This is logical, because if they aren't sprayed, the plants have to make more effort themselves to survive,' explains Hanne Lakkenborg Kristensen.

Many of the healthy substances that are good for us are part of the plant's immune system.

Using these old varieties is good for the health, but also means the food tastes better and has more variety.

The aim of the project is to get Danes to eat more bitter vegetables. A financial calculation based on the results of the hospital trial shows that it would be possible to save billions in healthcare costs every year simply by serving traditional, more bitter local variants.

'We have observed a recent upswell of interest in vegetables when people discover these other flavour variations. If this ultimately leads to people eating more vegetables, we've gained a great deal,' says Hanne Lakkenborg Kristensen.

Globally, foods with strong and often slightly bitter or tart flavours have been strongly associated with a healthy lifestyle. The Japanese island of Okinawa is well known for its cooking, and it's also the place on Earth where people live longest. The cornerstone in the local food culture consists of tart and slightly bitter ingredients such as goya, also known as bitter melon, hirami lemon, mugwort and a range of local herbs. Goya gets its bitter flavour from the substance berberine, which has a proven anti-cancer effect and has even been linked to positive effects for the heart and for blood sugar regulation.

The Italian village of Acciaroli, south of Salerno, is another of the places where people are known to live for a long time. Here, the average length of life for women is 92 – eight years longer than the Italian average – while the average for men is 85 years.

An ongoing study shows that the residents regularly wander around the rocky hillsides, picking wild and extremely flavourful herbs which are chock full of bioactive substances.

And the favourite herb in Acciaroli? Well, people here eat the traditional Mediterranean diet where they add large amounts of rosemary to almost all of their dishes. And rosemary, particularly in its raw form, has a strong flavour that's quite resinous.

On the Greek island of Ikaria, another of the blue zones where people regularly live to be 100, the residents also pick large quantities of rosemary, oregano and thyme, all of which grow wild on the rocky slopes. As I'm writing this, I get such a craving that I open a bag of mountain herbs I brought back with me from my latest visit, breathe in the scent and make a cup of tea.

Somehow, the herbs that grow on Ikaria smell more than the same herbs grown somewhere else. And strangely enough, they have more flavour if they come from the north-west of the island than from the south-east.

So that must be a question of *terroir*.

Rye – the seed of happiness

For a long time, rye was the most important cereal in Sweden and the rest of the Nordic countries. It now turns out that eating rye bread with whole grains for your evening snack can prevent obesity and Type 2 diabetes and also improve your mood the next morning. In a new PhD thesis, rye emerges as the perfect happiness food. Other results indicate that rye seems to have a delaying effect on Alzheimer's.

In many studies, whole grains have been shown to be good for the health, but are often brought into question as a result of their carbohydrate content.

'We want to know more about why whole grains are so good. My thesis gives still more arguments for why we should eat more whole grains, particularly rye and barley,' explains Jonna Sandberg when I ring to discuss the subject.

Possible causes are that whole rye grains reach right down into the colon without dissolving, and there they are fermented by the gut bacteria. This generates a number of substances that improve gut health,

reduce feelings of hunger and balance blood sugar fluctuations for 11–14 hours after the meal.

This is usually called the second-meal effect, because the blood sugar is kept down during the next meal too. The effect occurred when the whole grains were mixed with whole grain rye flour with added resistant starch.

Jonna works at the Department of Food Technology, Engineering and Nutrition at Lund University. Here, researchers have previously investigated how our metabolism and gut flora are affected positively by whole barley grains.

Rye is thought to play a similar

role. But there are differences. While rye affects feelings of satiety to a greater extent, barley has a slightly stronger effect on balancing the blood sugar.

The conclusion? That diversity is good. It's a good thing to eat whole grains from a range of cereals because they contain different fibre types. And don't forget oats, which, like barley, contain an additional type of healthy fibre: beta-glucans, which regulate feelings of satiety but also the body's secretion of insulin and blood sugar level. This may explain the ability of whole grains to prevent obesity and diabetes.

The positive effect of rye bread was clearly greatest when whole grains were included. This then constitutes a form of resistant starch that is protected by its hull and reaches further down into the gut before it is fermented by the gut bacteria. Finely ground whole grain flour doesn't have as good an effect, despite containing lots of fibre together with vitamins and minerals.

When participants were asked to mark on a scale whether they felt happy or depressed, satisfied or dissatisfied, passive or active, rye turned out to be the perfect happiness food.

But the most surprising discovery was that people eating rye bread for supper were in a better mood the following morning.

This particular finding is the first of its type, but imagine if that's the explanation why the Danish constantly come out as the world's happiest people. Because few people eat as much rye bread as the Danes!

Rye

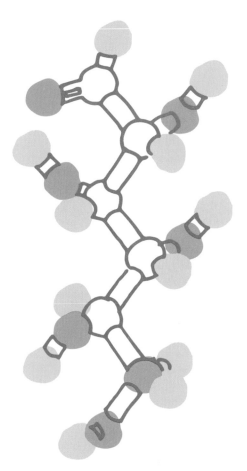

If instead there are many sugar molecules together, these are called polysaccharides. This is actually an umbrella term. It's under this that we first find starch, which is the plant's way of storing energy, and glycogen, which is the corresponding substance in people and animals.

The polysaccharides in food that are neither starch nor glycogen are dietary fibre.

The only thing that distinguishes polysaccharides chemically from normal sugar is that the sugar molecules form long chains.

When these chains are a little shorter, they can be snipped off by the body's own enzymes, so that the sugar molecules are ultimately small enough to be absorbed by the blood. This process begins in the mouth and continues in the small intestine.

The smaller the sugar molecules, the more quickly they are absorbed in the body. Fibre has such long chains that they aren't broken down at all by our own enzymes in the small intestine. Instead, they become food for the bacteria living in the colon.

In the fermentation process, fatty acids and other substances are created that we need and which balance blood sugar and counteracts inflammation in the gut.

Fibre – the crash course

OK, so it can be tricky to keep track of all the stuff we know about fibre. But the basics are really simple. Everything's sugar.

If it's a single sugar molecule, it's called a monosaccharide. Examples of these are glucose and fructose.

Glossary:
Carbohydrates

Glucose: Also called dextrose. Used as energy by muscle cells or stored in fat cells.

Fructose: Fruit sugar. Not stored in muscle or fat cells, but instead goes directly to the liver where it is converted into glucose. The level in fruit is relatively low.

Blood sugar: The level of glucose in the blood, which is measured in units of mmol per litre. Healthy people should have a blood sugar level of 4–7 mmol/l.

Ordinary table sugar: Glucose + fructose.

Starch: How plants store energy. Consists of long chains of glucose. Bread, pasta and potatoes are foods with lots of starch.

Glycogen: Glucose when it's stored in the liver.

Dietary fibre: Parts of plants that aren't broken down by our own enzymes in the stomach and small intestine, and which therefore reach the colon. They are broken down to varying extents by the gut bacteria.

Resistant starch: So stable that we used to believe it wasn't broken down in the gut at all. That's why it's not even called dietary fibre. Now we know it's excellent for gut health. Found in legumes, lentils and whole grains that still have their hull, together with green bananas and in raw or boiled potatoes which have been allowed to cool. The same applies to a certain extent to rice and pasta. The fibre effect of pasta is also better when it is eaten al dente – in other words, it's still a bit chewy. In reality, there are often many different types of fibre in individual ingredients. For example, both resistant starch and beta-glucans which are found in oats and barley, and even in mushrooms, nourish bacteria that produce butyric acid. This in turn contributes to good gut health and balanced blood sugar levels.

Remember: You don't really need to learn to distinguish between the different types of fibre. Instead remember to eat food made from whole ingredients. All ingredients contain a mixture of many different fibres. Then you just have to vary the ingredients.

What? Wheat

The disadvantages, such as gluten intolerance and the link to obesity and Type 2 diabetes, are well known. But is all wheat – and all ways of using wheat – equally harmful? Is there some way of avoiding the risks?

Few things can stimulate such an intensive discussion of food as a grain of wheat. And few foods are so two-faced. On one hand, it is an easily cultivated ingredient that has filled billions of stomachs – and on the other it is a symbol for Western junk food.

Despite the fact that our ancestors ground and ate wheat at least 30,000 years ago, wheat is linked to many of the health problems that have increased rapidly in recent years, such as obesity, diabetes and gut problems caused by gluten intolerance and gluten sensitivity.

The suspicion of wheat is above all based on four things.

1. *Carbohydrates*. White flour with fast carbohydrates increases blood sugar fluctuations and is linked to increased insulin resistance, obesity and Type 2 diabetes.

2. *Nutritional content.* In white flour, the healthiest parts, including the fibre, have been removed.

3. *Gluten.* The level of gluten in modern, intensively cultivated wheat types has meant that many people can't tolerate wheat.

4. Many seeds and legumes, including wheat, contain *phytic acid*, which counteracts the uptake of iron and other minerals.

We've already looked at the first two points. In modern mills with steel rollers, the wheat grain is transformed into a fine dust which means it is very rapidly absorbed in the small intestine and therefore leads to a high blood sugar spike.

But just as with other types of grain, the effect is completely different if we eat the whole or coarsely chopped whole grains.

They then retain their original content of minerals and bioactive substances, and also reach down into the colon without making the blood sugar spike.

Someone who knows a lot about grains – and not least about wheat – is Kerstin Fredlund, a doctor in food science, who wrote her PhD thesis about flour. She is involved in Allkorn, a project started in 1995 at the Swedish University of Agricultural Sciences to preserve old local types of grain. Kerstin Fredlund is worried about how today's fibre-poor grains are affecting public health, but she can also see solutions.

When we meet, she emphasises that all grains, including different types of wheat, come from wild grasses that have existed for more than 6 million years and have been important sources of food for the whole period during which human civilisation has developed.

'But humans have never previously eaten so few types as today,' says Fredlund, pointing out that this monotony is one of the really big problems. Since time began, our ancestors have been omnivores who have collected and eaten large quantities of different types of food. Archaeological finds show that this has involved meat, fish and many different types of plants, including seeds.

Today, a full 60% of all the energy eaten on the planet comes from four crops: wheat, rice, corn and potatoes.

Kerstin Fredlund works as a local doctor on the island of Öland, while simultaneously carrying on a stubborn battle to preserve our old heirloom grains and methods. In other words, she's that rare creature – a researcher and entrepreneur who develops products but also meets her own patients in a primary care context.

'It's become very common to have 60-year-olds coming in here with colon cancer, Type 2 diabetes and cardiovascular disease. These are lifestyle diseases that at least 2 million people in Sweden suffer from. Researchers are convinced that eating things like whole grains can prevent these diseases. But only one in ten of us eat enough whole grains.'

The lack of fibre in our diet is linked to the fact that for 100 years, sifted wheat flour has become our main source of grain. Wheat flour was initially the preserve of the upper classes, but in the early 1900s the unions fought to ensure that the working classes also had access to wheat flour. It was a symbol of the 'good life'.

'We're now harvesting the terrifying effects in terms of ill-health related to a lack of fibre. We need to eat far more fibre in Sweden today,' Fredlund says.

She points out that wheat cultivation has been aimed at high yields and that the industry wants wheat with good technical characteristics (such as resistance to insect attack, moisture and heat tolerance, good storage properties and so on) and a high gluten content to give it good baking properties. Modern wheat is tasteless compared to the old types, the ones that are called heirloom wheats.

'My dream is that the industry will start growing the old regional and heirloom varieties in a way that emphasises their flavour, colour and other characteristics. There's an enormous difference in aromas between the different types. And these differences should be exploited in the same way that they are for coffee and chocolate. The differences between different types of grain are just as important as grapes are in the production of wine!'

Kerstin Fredlund's message is that health problems can largely be managed effectively by learning from traditional but now often forgotten methods. In fact, that this isn't merely possible but even necessary.

As we all know, humanity is faced by enormous challenges when it comes to feeding a growing population while the cultivable land area is expected to reduce as a result of climate change. In such a position, it's difficult, particularly in some climate zones, to avoid grains which are both easy to cultivate and have a high nutrient density in the form of fibre that is good for the gut flora, protein and even vitamins and minerals. If it's only done the right way.

We look at gluten

Until the end of the 1800s, here in Sweden we ate many different varieties of barley, oats and rye, together with several different types of wheat such as einkorn wheat, emmer wheat, spelt and a range of landrace wheats. But in 100 years, we've lost three quarters of these seed types.

Today, modern wheat varieties constitute a large proportion of all calories consumed around the world.

'Consuming such a monotonous diet based on a few completely new types of wheat is a completely new phenomenon in human history,' says Kerstin Fredlund. 'I view it as a gigantic experiment with public health, without any control group.'

Gluten creates the threads that bind the dough together and make the bread rise and become fluffy. And of course these are desirable baking characteristics. Unfortunately, about one third of all people in Sweden, the rest of Europe and the USA carry genes that mean they risk developing Coeliac disease, or gluten intolerance. In Sweden, about 3% of the population suffer from the disease, which is a lifetime condition, and a further 10% suffer from gluten-related problems.

Studies have shown an increased risk for those with a disturbed gut flora, with a larger proportion of toxin-producing bacteria. In mice, gluten intolerance can be induced with antibiotics, and there is even an increased risk linked to other medicines, as well as viral infections suffered as a child and to caesarean sections.

Kerstin Fredlund believes many people aren't aware that gluten consists of several hundred different proteins that resemble each other but only a few of which produce the biggest damage.

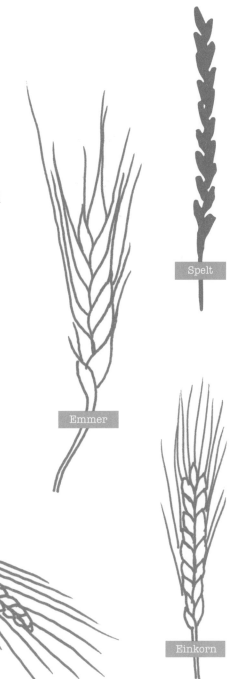

Spelt

Emmer

Khorasan

Einkorn

Gluten – the masterclass

Gluten primarily consists of what are known as prolamines and glutenines. In wheat, the prolamines are called gliadins, and one of these – alpha-gliadin – has been shown to play the biggest role in the development of gluten intolerance.

But not even all alpha-gliadin is equally harmful. There are 230 gene sequences, of which around 50 can be harmful and four in particular can damage the intestinal mucosa.

If we look at the total quantity of gluten, there's just as much or more in some older wheat varieties, such as spelt or other bread wheats. What these and modern wheat have in common is possessing 42 chromosomes. Primitive wheats such as einkorn wheat have only 14 chromosomes and low gluten strength.

Kerstin Fredlund explains that, just like durum wheat (the wheat used to make pasta), emmer wheat and kamut wheat have 28 chromosomes and a considerably smaller inflammatory effect on the gut compared with wheats with 42 chromosomes.

In rye, barley and oats, there are other prolamines, such as secalines, hordeines and avenines. These aren't as highly refined as modern wheat varieties. It's well known that the gluten in oats isn't harmful, and the impact of rye and barley gluten has not yet been fully investigated. But if you already have gluten intolerance, you can't eat these varieties of grains.

'Heirloom grains of different types contain a wider distribution of different gluten proteins, and the primitive einkorn and emmer wheat grains have a lower proportion of gluten with harmful epitopes (and thus a reduced ability to trigger a reaction in the immune system),' says Fredlund. 'If you've developed an intolerance to gluten, perhaps this won't be enough, but in groups of people who eat a number of different varieties, the problem doesn't seem to occur at all in the same way.'

An increased diversity of wheat types would probably mean that significantly fewer people will develop gluten intolerance from the outset. Just like it used to be.

In countries such as Italy and Germany, a large range of different grain types are sold, and gluten intolerance is less widespread than it is in Scandinavia. The number of people suffering from it is highest in the north European countries where the variation in grain types is low and sourdough fermentation less common.

During sourdough fermentation – ideally for more than 12 hours – or malting, the gluten proteins can be broken down fully or partially and such methods can therefore help reduce damage in the gut. However, this needs further investigation.

Kerstin Fredlund would also like to see an increased use of barley, rye and oats which all have their own special strengths and weaknesses in baking and food preparation.

If you want to continue to eat wheat but reduce your gluten intake, one tip is to choose einkorn wheat, emmer wheat, durum wheat or kamut wheat (Khorasan wheat). To vary the consumption, you can also choose spelt or other landrace wheats.

'Not least for things like porridge, bread, crispbread, pies, waffles, pancakes and baking. With less gluten, you need to learn another baking technique as it isn't as easy to bake with these wheat varieties,' Fredlund explains.

The bread is more compact, like it used to be. We've only relatively recently become accustomed to today's fluffy bread.

In Denmark, there's a traditional dish called øllebrød, which involves grating and making porridge out of sourdough bread and whole grain flour. Kerstin Fredlund says this makes great baby food.

Heirloom wheats can be found in the form of whole grains or groats in some shops. In Italy these are called 'farro' and are widely used in cookery in regions such as Umbria.

Hopefully, local versions of these types of groats will soon be more widely available in shops in other countries.

A little farming history

According to archaeologists, agriculture became a widespread practice around 12,000 years ago, but by then people had long been collecting wild grasses to eat.

Discoveries show that people were using stone tools 30,000 years ago to grind various types of nutritious grass seeds which they collected and stored. Advanced genetic analyses recently revealed that humans must have spent time growing wheat as early as 25,000 years ago.

Einkorn wheat: Has existed for 6.5 million years and is considered to be the first wild wheat that our ancestors ate, and then began to cultivate. It isn't a genetic relative of modern wheat. Einkorn wheat contains very little gluten, but it's still not considered to be safe for anyone who's already developed gluten intolerance. Contains a great deal of protein and carotenoids such as lutein and lycopene, which makes the flour yellowish.

Emmer wheat: Has existed for 380,000 years. This is also an original wheat but one that's a relative of the modern types. Typically these have a noticeable

flavour and are darker in colour than modern wheat. Emmer wheat dominated cultivation for several thousand years around the eastern Mediterranean. Einkorn wheat and emmer wheat were cultivated in Scandinavia as much as 5,000 years ago and until the Viking Age, but were abandoned as the climate turned colder. Until the 1900s, barley, rye and oats then dominated.

Spelt wheat: Spelt arose several hundred thousand years ago as a cross between emmer wheat and wild grass. It was first cultivated around 7,000 years ago and soon arrived in Sweden where it was grown until the Viking Age. The flavour is quite mild. Spelt is a hulled grain and contains as much pro-inflammatory gluten as modern bread wheats.

Durum wheat: Derived from emmer wheat, with the big difference that durum has no hull so it doesn't have to be hulled after threshing.

Kamut wheat (also called Khorasan wheat): Developed from emmer wheat but its grains are twice the size of a modern wheat kernel, and have a nutty flavour. Kamut probably originates in Anatolia, but was then cultivated in Egypt several thousand years ago. According to legend, the grain was found during an early excavation of a Pharaoh's tomb, but the species was probably also grown locally in the Middle East. It became known to the rest of the world in 1949 when an American pilot took Egyptian seeds home with him to Montana, where commercial cultivation began in the 1970s.

Landrace wheat: Naked wheat species without hulls arose through cross-fertilisation of emmer wheat and wild grass. More recent research shows that naked bread wheats existed several thousand years before hulled spelt wheat. Different types of landrace wheats have developed and adapted to the local environment and climate. Spelt and landrace wheats contain a lot of protein and carotenoids such as lutein and lycopene which gives the fields of wheat a golden shimmer.

Barley: Just like wheat, barley evolved out of wild grass species and, together with einkorn wheat and emmer wheat, was one of the first grains cultivated by humans.

Rye: A grass cultivated in Central Europe 3,500 years ago. Rye was long the most important bread grain in Sweden, but use has dropped enormously in the last 100 years.

Oats: Have been grown in Europe for 2,000 years and in the 1800s represented half of all bread grain grown in Sweden.

Oats

195

Contrary minerals

Perhaps just as big a problem as gluten intolerance, but one that's received less attention, is that all grains contain phytic acid. The more minerals, the more phytic acid. This prevents the uptake of important minerals such as iron and zinc but also magnesium, potassium, phosphorus and manganese.

Phytic acid is also found in legumes, nuts and oil seeds. Nuts and seeds that are eaten raw also contain an enzyme that helps neutralise the phytic acid in the gut.

In developing countries, among the poorest people, who have abandoned their traditional diet, a few staple foods often represent a large proportion of their nutrition. In such groups, the phytic acid in grains can cause major problems and contribute to a deficiency of minerals and malnutrition. This is known as hidden starvation. In the Western world, despite concerns mentioned on a number of blogs, this problem has been more limited because most people obtain sufficient iron and zinc when they eat meat. Because the uptake from animal products is not affected by phytic acid.

While a quarter of the iron in meat is absorbed by the body, only around 5% of the iron in seeds is absorbed.

The industry has chosen to counteract the problem by enriching the flour with minerals. This may sound clever but can lead to new problems. For example, it's a waste of resources to cultivate and eat mineral-rich food that we can't make use of.

There are also some uncertainties relating to the uptake of the iron used in such enrichment. Only 2-3% of this added iron is absorbed. A number of researchers, including Kerstin Fredlund, say that it has not yet been demonstrated that iron enrichment is harmless. Because iron is a pro-oxidant, the remaining iron enables unfavourable gut

bacteria to flourish, which can increase the risk of cancer.

A better idea, according to these researchers, is for the grain industry to employ large scale versions of methods similar to those used by our ancestors, namely to break down the phytic acid and increase the biological uptake of minerals through sourdough, sprouting, malting, soaking and heat treatment.

In the 1990s, Kerstin Fredlund was involved in a patent taken out for the Swedish grain industry. But despite internal support, the project lacked backing at the highest level. The patent was never used and when it recently expired, Fredlund founded a company, Hidden in Grains, in the hope of being able to bring the ideas to fruition, even on a very small scale.

Today the issue has become extra relevant. Many people want to reduce the amount of meat they eat, and for vegetarians and vegans it's important to take care to avoid a deficiency of iron and other minerals. But what actually is phytic acid? It's intended to protect the seed's phosphorus, enabling it to grow. But the chemical link is so strong that our bodies also have problems absorbing the other minerals in the seed.

Phytic acid can also slow the uptake of minerals from other food eaten at the same time. It has no permanent effect, but instead seems only to affect uptake from what you're eating at that time.

This doesn't mean that you have to avoid whole grains and only eat meat to get sufficient minerals in your diet.

Whole grains are so healthy in so many other ways that it's a bad idea to completely exclude them from your diet. This would mean that you would also miss out on all the other great things they contain: fibre, vitamins, oils and lots of different bioactive substances. And remember: many studies are unequivocal about the fact that people who eat nuts and whole grains are healthier and live longer.

Nuts and seeds can also be eaten raw and this preserves an enzyme that means the phytic acid is broken down in the gut.

The benefit is quite clearly greater than the risks. You simply have to look at the people around the world who live the longest and healthiest lives: they all have foods that contain phytic acid on the menu. The secret seems to lie in using a few simple tricks.

Historically, humans have never eaten grains raw or unprocessed. It's no coincidence that soaking, sourdough fermentation and sprouting, but also various moisture and heat treatments of grains and legumes have been among the traditional culinary arts since time began. All of these methods break down the phytic acid wholly or partially and release the minerals, which can be absorbed in the gut.

The easiest way to break down the phytic acid is to use nature's own manual and activate the enzyme phytase, which is also found naturally in seeds.

Soaking: In legumes and whole grains, phytic acid can be broken down by soaking them overnight. If the industry introduced soaking and heating of grains to just above 50°C as a standard process, the problem would to a large extent disappear. An acidic environment improves the activity of phytase. So you should add something sour such as lemon juice or vinegar to the soaking water.

Sprouting: When the seed sprouts, phytase is activated and phytic acid is broken down, because the seed uses phosphorus when it sprouts, making the minerals available.

Sourdough fermentation – ideally for more than 12 hours – is another way of making the minerals available in bread. The acidic environment created by the lactic acid bacteria promotes the breakdown of phytic acid.

There are more tricks, too: If you make sure that the same meal involves you consuming vitamin C from something like oranges or berries, such as blackcurrants, sea buckthorn, rosehips or even kiwi fruit, you increase your iron uptake. This takes place by means of the iron being chemically altered from what is known as trivalent iron to bivalent iron.

Iron must always be in bivalent form to be absorbed. In all plants, iron is initially trivalent, unlike in animals. As well as vitamin C, organic acids such as those found in lactic fermented vegetables also increase iron uptake. So when you sprinkle nuts or seeds on your muesli or salad, why not top it off with berries, kiwi fruit or oranges?

Tannins in coffee and tea can also obstruct mineral uptake, but these too are counteracted by vitamin C.

Vitamin C bombs

Vitamin C has been known for so long that we tend to forget about it, despite all its health advantages. There are many good sources of vitamin C.

Vitamin C can be found in the majority of fruit and vegetables, and a deficiency is now quite rare. But if you eat little or no meat – which facilitates mineral uptake – and at the same time a lot of nuts, seeds and whole grains, a little extra vitamin C can reinforce your uptake of iron, zinc, calcium and other minerals that make you and your body feel better.

The daily dose recommended by health authorities (80 micrograms) corresponds to either one large orange, a third of a red pepper, 100 grams broccoli or three Brussels sprouts.

Some people think we need significantly more vitamin C than that. Double Nobel prizewinner Linus Pauling observed that people, other primates and guinea pigs are the only animals that can't produce their own vitamin C. When he compared a human diet with what primates eat, he determined that we ought to eat at least 1,000mg per day. This is still a controversial opinion, but even more recent studies also indicate the benefit of eating food that contains lots of vitamin C.

Vitamin C is heat sensitive and can reduce significantly if food is heated for a long period or reheated several times. And, for example, unpeeled boiled potatoes retain more vitamin C than peeled ones do.

Orange: (53mg per 100 grams) Eat the whole fruit so you get the fibre too and not just the fruit juice. Alternate with lemon, lime and grapefruit.

Guava: (182mg per 100 grams) Other exotic fruit also have high levels of vitamin C, such as kiwi fruit (63mg) and papaya (62mg).

Rosehip: High levels but hard to eat. The proportion of vitamin C is highest in rosehips, with more than 400mg per 100 grams. In second place is chilli peppers. But rosehips have to be dried, boiled into tea or made into soup. (Rosehip soup: 190mg per 100 grams)

Blackcurrant: (150mg per 100 grams) Among the traditional berries, blackcurrants are best for vitamin C, closely followed by redcurrants. Sea buckthorn, blueberries and cloudberries, together with raspberries and strawberries, are also good alternatives.

Kale: (120mg per 100 grams) Of course, the plant kingdom's answer to a multivitamin tablet also contains vitamin C. Alternate with red cabbage, Brussels sprouts, broccoli, white cabbage and cauliflower.

Sugar snap peas: (66mg per 100 grams) Some legumes are an excellent source of vitamin C. The most is found in sugar snap peas, followed by broad beans, green beans and wax beans.

Red pepper: (205mg per 100 grams) On one hand, red peppers are tasty and full of healthy bioactive substances such as vitamin C. On the other hand, red peppers are among the vegetables that are most sprayed, and with the most pesticides. Organic is best.

Parsley: (182mg per 100 grams) A large number of herbs contain high levels of vitamin C, not least parsley and thyme. But rosemary, coriander, basil, dill and chives are also good sources. Fresh and frozen work just as well provided they're frozen soon after being picked. Dried herbs and berries, together with dried fruit also retain many of the bioactive substances, but the volatile vitamin C can reduce somewhat.

Boiled potatoes: (14mg per 100 grams) In practice, an important source of vitamin C for anyone who eats too little fruit and vegetables. Horseradish, kohlrabi, Hamburg parsley and celeriac also contain reasonable levels of vitamin C. And there's a bit in carrots too.

Feel good minerals

A vegetarian diet is good for the health in many ways but increases the risk of a deficiency of some minerals and vitamins, which in turn affects how we feel mentally. Fortunately, this can be counteracted.

Iron deficiency affects almost one in four Swedish women of fertile age. Even if iron deficiency doesn't directly cause depression, it can produce symptoms such as headaches, fatigue, mood swings and concentration difficulties. Iron deficiency can also cause an irregular heartbeat, which can lead to anxiety and panic attacks. Vitamin C, for example from citrus fruit, improves uptake.

Zinc is the next most common mineral in the brain after iron and is the mineral most clearly linked to depression. The nature of the symptoms is related to the severity of the deficiency. Studies show that zinc supplements can speed recovery when given as a complement to other treatment. Red meat and shellfish are important sources.

Magnesium and depression have a long shared history of reported connections. Studies have had varying results, but a number show that a deficiency increases the risk of depression and that supplements have a positive effect. Stress means that your stores of magnesium are depleted more quickly. Uptake is counteracted by calcium, which many people get a lot of. One solution is to eat a varied diet including whole grains, nuts and seeds.

Selenium deficiency has also been shown to have a connection with depression, but this is not entirely unequivocal and is weaker than for both zinc and magnesium. In countries such as Sweden, where the levels of selenium in the soil are low, we get less via grains than in countries with soils that are richer in selenium. Selenium is a powerful antioxidant that protects sensitive polyunsaturated fatty acids in the cells from oxidising. Selenium also helps during production of thyroid hormones that give us energy and vitality. Selenium is found in foods including nuts, whole grains, beef and offal. Uptake doesn't seem to be as strongly affected by phytic acid.

Iodine deficiency disrupts the thyroid, which in turn affects everything from energy and metabolism to immune system and brain function. One of the symptoms can be depression. In Sweden, iodine deficiency was once common but that changed when table salt was enriched with iodine. Now that many people are instead choosing mineral-rich rock and sea salt, this has paradoxically resulted in an increasing level of iodine deficiency.

B vitamins, and above all folate and vitamin B12, have been shown to reduce the symptoms of depression in several double blind studies. The best source of B12 is meat, which is why vegetarians may require a supplement. But B12 is also produced by the gut bacteria. Folate can be found in foods including beans, whole grains and leafy green vegetables. The sources are largely the same as for magnesium.

Omega-3 fats, which are found in oily fish such as herring, salmon and mackerel, have been shown to help a majority of those being treated for depression. But more studies are required. It's above all the fatty acids EPA and DHA that have a positive effect. Omega-3 fats contain vital fatty acids that we can only obtain from food. The majority of us get far too little of these fats, which is why we are recommended to eat fish several times a week. Omega-3 fats also have a beneficial effect on the gut flora.

Øllebrød

To use up old rye bread, Danish monks once made porridge out of the leftovers. Now it turns out that rye contains extremely nutritious fibre. This is a combination that has rapidly transformed øllebrød into a fine dining experience in several of the world's best restaurants. And it also tastes great! It can be flavoured with lemon or orange, or as here with a delicious egg cream.

4 slices of rye bread
approx. 200ml water, to cover
3 tablespoons sugar
1 egg

1. Break the bread into smaller pieces and cover with water. Leave to stand for 1 hour.
2. Place in a saucepan and allow to cook for 5–8 minutes over a low heat. Mix the entire time until you obtain a creamy consistency.
3. Add 2 tablespoons of the sugar and blend until smooth in a food processor or with a stick blender.
4. Whisk the egg and remaining sugar until fluffy with an electric whisk.
5. Serve the egg cream with the warm porridge.

Three types of bread

People have been baking bread for at least 14,400 years. In 2018, a bread oven was discovered that was used 4,000 years before agriculture became widespread. How is that possible? Our ancestors collected wild seeds, which gave them a wide variety of types, far from today's monotonous and fibre-poor consumption which triggers intolerances. The process of sourdough fermentation is also known to make the minerals in the bread available to our bodies.

Crispbread with potatoes
15–20 pieces

Step 1
750ml milk
150g butter, melted
5 tablespoons honey
25g yeast
500g sifted rye flour
500g wheat flour, ideally organic
    and stoneground

Step 2
1 tablespoon salt
500g graham flour
500g wheat flour
750g boiled, peeled almond
    potatoes

1. Heat the milk, butter and honey to about 37°C – hand hot.
2. Dissolve the yeast in the lukewarm liquid and add the rye and wheat flour.
3. Knead into a smooth dough, by hand or with a food processor.
4. Leave to rise under a tea towel at room temperature or slightly warmer for about 45 minutes.
5. Preheat the oven to 250°C and use a baking stone if you have one.
6. Add salt, graham flour and wheat flour. Knead into the dough.
7. Mash the potatoes and add to the dough. Continue to knead until the potatoes are evenly distributed.
8. Roll out thinly into sheets that you can easily handle and which will fit into the oven.
9. Place the dough onto the baking stone or baking sheet, and cook for 2-4 minutes per side.
10. Leave to cool on a rack.

Sourdough bread

2 loaves

Step 1: Sourdough starter

400ml lukewarm water, 37°C
320g wheat flour, ideally organic
   and stoneground
1 tablespoon honey

Step 2: Bread

25g yeast
600ml water, room temperature
900g wheat flour, ideally organic
   and stoneground
400g sourdough starter
   (see recipe)
5 teaspoons salt

Day 1-2 – Sourdough starter

1. Mix 200ml of water, 150g of flour and the honey. Whisk until smooth.
2. Pour into a bowl with a lid or cover with clingfilm. Leave to stand at room temperature for 2 days.

Day 3 – Sourdough starter

3. Add 100ml of water and 85g of flour to the mixture and whisk until smooth. Cover again and leave to stand for another day.

Day 4 – Sourdough starter

4. Repeat the process for Day 3.

Day 5 – Bake the bread

5. Dissolve the yeast in the water. Add half of the flour and knead the dough for 10 minutes.
6. Add the sourdough starter, salt and the remaining flour, and knead the dough for a further 20 minutes.
7. Place the dough in a bowl and leave to rise under a tea towel for 2 hours.
8. Turn out the dough onto a floured worktop, divide it in two and carefully form two loaves. Avoid overworking the dough to retain as much air in it as possible.
9. Sprinkle a little flour over and cover with a tea towel. Leave to rise for a further 1½ hours.
10. Preheat the oven to 250°C. Use a baking stone if you have one, or otherwise an upside down baking tray. Place in the oven to warm.
11. Place a small saucepan or heat-resistant bowl in the oven, with a couple of centimetres of water in the bottom.
12. Place the bread on the stone or baking sheet in the oven.
13. Reduce the oven temperature to 200°C and bake for 40-50 minutes. The bread is ready when it sounds hollow if you tap it. Leave to cool on a rack.

Emmer flour baguette

6 baguettes

Step 1: Poolish

800g wheat flour, ideally organic
   and stoneground
20g yeast, fresh
1 litre water, cold

Step 2: Baguette

600g wheat flour, ideally organic
   and stoneground
2 tablespoons sea salt
200g emmer flour

Day 1 – Poolish

1. Mix the flour, yeast and water
    until you obtain a thick pancake-
    type batter.
2. Cover with a baking mat or tea
    towel. Leave to stand at room
    temperature for 12–16 hours,
    until it has doubled in volume.

Day 2 – Bake the bread

3. Pour out the wheat flour in a
    heap on your worktop. Scoop out
    100–200g flour and set aside.
4. Make a hollow in the flour and
    pour in the poolish and sea salt.
5. Stir the poolish with one hand,
    and with the other incorporate
    a little emmer flour at a time
    until the dough has bound
    together. Top up with the wheat
    flour you set to one side, if
    necessary. The dough should
    feel smooth and not sticky.
6. Shape the dough into a ball,
    cover with a tea towel and leave
    to rise for 30 minutes.
7. Divide into 6 equal pieces.
8. Cover with a tea towel and leave
    to rest for a further 10 minutes.
9. Form the dough into baguettes.

Don't overwork the dough; you
want to keep as much air in it
as possible.

10. Place onto a baking sheet,
    leaving space for the baguettes
    to rise. Sprinkle with a little
    flour and cover with a tea towel.
11. Leave to rise for 3–4 hours.
12. Preheat the oven to 260°C.
13. Make diagonal cuts in the top
    surface of the baguette and
    bake in the oven for 20–25
    minutes.
14. Leave to cool on a rack for
    about 30 minutes.

Mackerel sandwich

Like all fatty fish, mackerel is full of healthy Omega-3 fats. Why is that so good? Well to start with, about half of your brain's grey cells consist of the fish fat DHA, which you have to take in through food – your body can't manufacture it. So you can actually affect the size of your brain with good food, such as mackerel.

200–300g smoked mackerel
2 tablespoons capers
4 tablespoons mayonnaise
5cm leek, sliced
1 tablespoon lemon juice
1 tablespoon grated horseradish
2 baguettes (see page 207)
olive oil
4 eggs
1 bunch of chard leaves or lettuce

1. Remove the bones from the smoked mackerel and flake the fish into smaller pieces.
2. Mix the mackerel, capers, mayonnaise, leek, lemon juice and grated horseradish.
3. Divide the bread lengthways and toast under a grill, drizzled with a little olive oil.
4. Meanwhile, heat a little olive oil in a frying pan over a medium heat. Carefully break the eggs into the pan and fry for 2-3 minutes until the whites are set.
5. Top the bread with the mackerel mix, fried egg and chard.
6. Grate a little extra horseradish and squeeze lemon juice over.

Skyr with Nordic berries and seeds

Icelandic skyr was originally
made from unpasteurised
milk direct from the cow.
After this, a splash of old
skyr was added to get the
right lactic acid bacteria,
which kept away other
microbes. It could then keep
through the entire winter.
The Swedish and Finnish
equivalent is sour milk, but
in today's microbe-phobic
world an acidic culture
of pasteurised milk is
often added.

200ml skyr
200–300g Nordic berries
   (blackberries, blackcurrants,
   blueberries)
3 tablespoons sunflower seeds
2 tablespoons honey

1. Top the skyr with berries, seeds
    and honey.

Beansprouts with seeds and lentils

Nature has an excellent system where the seeds protect their minerals until it's time to sprout. Sprouting releases iron and other minerals so that we can more easily absorb them. We absorb a fair amount anyway because seeds contain high levels of minerals, but for vegans in particular it can be useful to think of your levels. There are several ways to fool the seed, such as sourdough baking or combining seeds with citrus fruit.

Sprouted chickpeas

1. Soak 200g dried chickpeas for 12 hours.
2. Rinse the starch off with cold water.
3. Place in a large glass jar.
4. Cover with a thin cloth and fasten in place with a rubber band. Store in a dark place at room temperature.
5. Rinse in cold water twice a day. After 2-3 days, they will start to sprout.
6. After 5-6 days they will be ready to eat.

Sprouted green lentils

1. Soak 100g green lentils for 8 hours.
2. Rinse the starch off with cold water.
3. Place in a large glass jar.
4. Cover with a thin cloth and fasten in place with a rubber band. Store in a dark place at room temperature.
5. Rinse in cold water twice a day. After 2-3 days, they will start to sprout.

6. After 5 days, they're ready to eat.

Sprouted sunflower seeds

1. Soak 100g dried sunflower seeds for 2 hours.
2. Rinse the starch off with cold water.
3. Place in a large glass jar.
4. Cover with a thin cloth and fasten in place with a rubber band. Store in a dark place at room temperature.
5. Rinse in cold water twice a day. After 3 days, they will start to sprout.
6. After 4 days, they're ready to eat.

Buckwheat risotto with fennel and pea sprout salad

Fennel is the slightly neglected cousin of parsley and coriander. The seeds and stalk have both been used in natural medicine, and fennel's fibre and folate content have given it a reputation as being good for the heart. Here it's served with beetroot, which has a vasodilating effect, and naturally gluten-free buckwheat. Västerbottensost cheese isn't only really tasty, it was also one of Henrik's ancestors who discovered it. If you can't source västerbottensost, then aged Cheddar cheese will work too.

2 shallots
300g crushed buckwheat
3 tablespoons cold-pressed
    rapeseed oil
600ml chicken stock
150g Västerbottensost cheese
    (or aged Cheddar cheese)
4 tablespoons crème fraîche
1 tablespoon fennel seeds
1 bulb of fennel
3–5 cooked beetroot
pea sprouts or green leaves or
    herbs, such as basil or oregano,
    to serve

1. Peel and chop the shallots.
2. Sauté the shallots and buckwheat in the rapeseed oil for 4–5 minutes in a wide, thick-bottomed saucepan.
3. Stir and add the chicken stock, a little at a time. Allow the liquid to reduce and add more stock while stirring until there's still a little bite in the buckwheat.
4. Grate half of the cheese into the pan and add the crème fraîche.
5. Toast the fennel seeds in a pan over a medium heat.
6. Thinly slice the fennel – this is easiest on a mandoline.
7. Cut the cooked beetroot into wedges.
8. Top the buckwheat risotto with toasted fennel seeds, sliced fresh fennel and beetroot. Shave the rest of the cheese over.
9. Add a few pea sprouts, green leaves or herbs.

Herring, asparagus and poached egg

Freshly caught Baltic herring, fried in a little butter on the boat. What could be nicer? But if you need a healthy reason to try it, each fish contains as much Omega-3 fat as an expensive capsule. All that remains is to tuck in, as my father-in-law used to say.

12–16 whole Baltic herring
spirit vinegar, 12%
4 eggs
12–16 green asparagus spears
3 tablespoons butter
2 tablespoons chopped shallots
1 tablespoon grated horseradish
3 teaspoons coarse grain mustard
salt

1. Cut open the abdomen of the herring, remove the guts and rinse in cold water. Place on kitchen paper to drain. Sprinkle over 1 tablespoon of salt.
2. Boil 2 litres of water in a wide saucepan. Add 2 tablespoons of spirit vinegar and 2 tablespoons of salt.
3. Break one egg at a time into a glass. Remove the boiling water from the heat and vigorously swirl the water until a vortex forms in the centre.
4. Add one egg at a time, continuing to swirl the water, and allow the egg to coagulate.
5. Test whether the egg is ready by lifting it out with a spoon and pressing it carefully. It should have a creamy yolk and a firm white. Place on kitchen paper to drain.

6. Break off the lowest part of the asparagus (peel if the shoots aren't tender).
7. Grill over a high heat or fry in a dry frying pan for 2–3 minutes per side. Set to one side.
8. Thoroughly heat a cast iron pan and fry the herring for 2–3 minutes on each side.
9. In a separate pan, melt the butter, add the chopped shallots, 2 teaspoons of spirit vinegar, the grated horseradish and mustard.
10. Serve the herring with asparagus and poached egg. Drizzle over the butter and mustard vinaigrette.

Note! If it's the season for ramsons, you can top this with both flowers and leaves.

'Får i kål': Lamb with cabbage and mustard seed

When I was growing up, the sheep breeders on the island of Öland insisted that their sheep tasted best because they flavoured themselves by grazing all their lives on the island's many wild herbs. I think that might well be true. And at the same time, they contribute to maintaining an open landscape and ecological diversity.

12–16 lamb chops (or saddle or fillet of lamb)
½ Savoy cabbage
20g mustard seeds
100ml spirit vinegar, 12%
200g sugar
300ml water
2 red onions
2 apples
butter, for frying
1 tablespoon honey
6 sprigs of thyme
salt and black pepper, freshly ground

1. Remove the lamb chops from the refrigerator 30 minutes before frying to temper the meat.
2. Boil about 2 litres of water with 2 tablespoons of salt.
3. Pick off the best leaves of the Savoy cabbage and cut out the stem from the middle.
4. Cook the cabbage leaves until soft in the boiling water (20–30 seconds). Cool in iced water.
5. Place the mustard seeds, spirit vinegar, sugar and water in a saucepan. Boil and allow to simmer for 20 minutes. Sieve out the pickled mustard seeds.
6. Peel the red onions. Cut the onions and apple into wedges. Fry them in butter in a hot pan until golden. Finish by adding the honey and thyme. Fry for 1 minute, then remove from the heat.
7. Season the lamb chops with salt and freshly ground black pepper.
8. Heat a large frying pan and fry the lamb chops in butter for 2–3 minutes per side or more if you prefer (it's important not to cover the entire surface of the pan – fry in batches if necessary).
9. Place the lamb chops on a dish and set aside for 4–5 minutes.
10. Heat the cabbage with 1 tablespoon of water and a knob of butter and then stir in the pickled mustard seeds.
11. Serve the cabbage with the lamb chops, onion and apple.

Bone marrow stock

Slow cooking was once done with the bone still in the stew, so the trend for bone marrow stock is nothing new. Bone marrow also contains the highest concentration of protein, minerals and fat-soluble vitamins. It's a great source of glucosamine, which helps the body restore cartilage, minerals such as calcium and magnesium that strengthen the skeleton, and the amino acid glycine, which is considered to have a calming effect.

2kg marrowbone
approx. 3 litres water
2 tablespoons apple cider vinegar
2 onions
½ head of garlic
4 carrots
½ leek
3 bay leaves
6 sprigs of thyme
10 black peppercorns

1. Preheat the oven to 200°C.
2. Roast the marrowbone in the oven for 40–50 minutes, turning halfway through.
3. Place the roasted bone in a saucepan. Cover with water and add the vinegar. Leave to stand for 30 minutes.
4. Boil and allow to simmer for 2 hours, skimming from time to time.
5. Peel the onions, garlic and carrots. Cut into largeish pieces, approx. 3 x 3cm.
6. Add all the vegetables and spices to the saucepan.
7. Continue to simmer over a very low heat or place in the oven at 95°C for 48 hours.
8. Sieve, and discard the bones.
9. Heat the stock carefully when serving or using for other recipes.

BACK TO YOUR ROOTS

CHAPTER 14

Fungi – we follow the guiding thread

Our view of fungi is in the process of changing quite significantly. In a short time, fungi have become one of the most trendy healthy ingredients, and are being added to everything from food to coffee, smoothies and stock.

For thousands of years, fungi have been a basic ingredient in every medicine man or woman's arsenal, but in modern times they've often been neglected as tasty but lacking nutrients.

There are two reasons for the recent interest:

Fungi contain a huge quantity of fibre that we can't ingest ourselves. This used to be considered as evidence that it was pointless to eat fungi. Now we know that this fibre provides food for our gut flora. And fungi contain lots of fibre – up to 60% dry weight.

Bioactive substances found in many types of fungi are now actively being investigated as ways of reinforcing the immune system and counteracting cardiovascular disease, cancer and dementia. New findings indicate that the substances in fungi affect the nervous system by protecting and reinforcing the brain neurons.

Despite the hype, however, we must remember that studies of how fungi affect the health are a long way behind the corresponding investigations for vegetables, berries and herbs.

But a few things have already been observed, such as the fact that fungi provide a useful source of protein and also contain minerals, including selenium, manganese, zinc, calcium and iron.

But – a note of caution here! – remember that if you're collecting fungi in the countryside you need to know what you're doing. The majority of fungi aren't edible and some are actually lethal. Even edible fungi often need to be blanched, boiled or fried.

Beta-glucans in fungi

Fungi are a very good source of beta-glucans, the type of fibre that occurs in oats and barley. Numerous studies have shown that these strengthen the immune system, reduce inflammation, counteract toxic bacteria and viruses, balance blood fats and blood sugar and even combat cancer.

There are varying levels of beta-glucans in fungi, but more in those that grow wild than cultivated ones. And the levels are often higher in the stalk than in the cap.

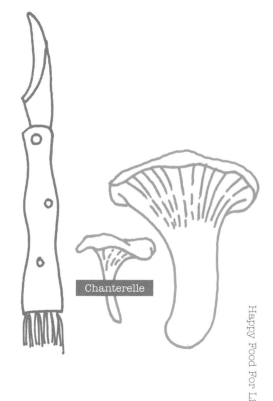

Chanterelle

Porcini – the king of the forest

Porcini mushrooms aren't merely one of the fungi that contain the most beta-glucans. A study presented in 2017 showed that porcini, followed by hen of the woods or maitake, have high levels of two very strong antioxidants, which many researchers say can have a very important effect on human health.

While porcini, followed by Pleurotus citrinopileatus, the golden oyster mushroom, was top of the list when it came to one of these (the amino acid ergothioneine), hen of the woods contained a little more of the other antioxidant (glutathione).

High levels of both are also found in oyster mushrooms and king trumpet mushrooms, while levels were lower in normal fungi such as chanterelles, white mushrooms, Agaricus silvaticus and portobello mushrooms. But even these contained higher levels than the majority of other foods.

Glutathione is an antioxidant found inside the cells and which has been shown to be important in the body's immune system, not least when it comes to handling carcinogenic substances.

The antioxidant effect of ergothioneine has long been known, and it has been suggested that the substance should be given the status of a vitamin. Above all, it collects in the organs that need the most defence, such as the blood, liver, kidneys and bone marrow. Biologically, the substance seems to have ancient roots in our bodies and to constitute a type of lifeguard that defends the cells' power stations – the mitochondria – from radiation.

It's possible that we and fungi went our separate evolutionary ways 650 million years ago – this seems far-fetched, but means we have similarities in our basic genetic functions – which is why this protective effect can probably be linked to our shared past.

It's interesting that the more we learn, the clearer it becomes that we are an inseparable part of all life on this planet, including fungi. The more we understand how it works and how everything hangs together, the greater are our chances not merely of surviving as a species but also of doing so with our bodies and minds full of happiness and energy.

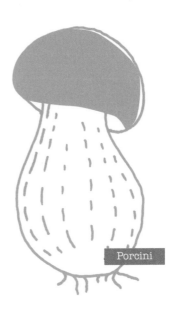

Porcini

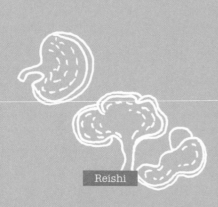

Reishi

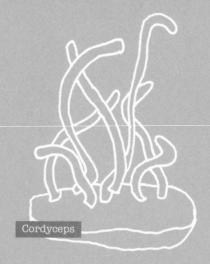

Cordyceps

Fact:
Fashionable superfungi

Inonotus obliquus (Chaga):
Perhaps the most hyped of all
'health' fungi. Contains high levels
of antioxidants and has long been
used as a natural remedy in Russia.
Anti-inflammatory.

**Hericium erinaceus (Lion's
mane):** Has long been used to
reinforce the immune system.
Common edible fungus in Asia
but endangered in Europe.

Cordyceps: Traditionally used
in China. Reinforces the immune
system and counteracts the stress
hormone cortisol. Is claimed to
increase oxygen uptake ability.

Lingzhi (Reishi): Is said to have
been used in China for 2,000
years. Lowers blood pressure,
reduces stress and is good for
sleep problems.

Note! Remember that in
Sweden, the chaga fungus
is not covered by the
right to roam and may
not be picked without the
landowner's consent.

Note! These four fungi are
rare and primarily sold
in powder form as health
foods. But new research
shows that many other
fungi too have a positive
impact, including porcini,
chanterelles, oyster
mushrooms, shiitake,
hen of the woods and
even normal white and
portobello (large brown)
mushrooms.

226

Getting started

You've probably had several light bulb moments while you've been reading this book. Some of these have perhaps given rise to still more questions, because we don't have all the answers yet. But what we do know is enough to get started.

Perhaps you've noticed that many of the new findings now being presented agree with the eating habits of traditional cultures where people are known for their good health. We think this is good. It provides evidence that what Niklas and I describe in this book has worked for many of the longest-lived people on our planet.

The important message to remember is simply this: don't eat a boring diet. Eat lots of different foods. This means that you consume different types of fibre, giving the biggest chance that all of your bacteria will continue to be happy and friendly and will want to stay with you.

The more types of gut bacteria you have, the more stable your gut flora – and the better you'll feel. Try not to exclude any ingredient completely.

We used to say: eat fruit and vegetables, and ideally leafy green vegetables. Today we know that we can be more accurate with this recommendation. We have drawn up a check list that you can use to make meals that are perfect, not just for you, but also for your microbes.

Basic ingredients – include something from each main group:

Legumes: kidney beans, black beans, common beans, mung beans or other beans; yellow and green peas, chickpeas, lentils.

Whole grain (cooked, whole or coarsely chopped): barley, oats, rye, buckwheat, millet, quinoa, brown rice, teff, popcorn. NB! You should ideally vary between barley, oats and rye, as they each contain different types of fibre. If you aren't gluten-intolerant, you can do as people used to long ago and alternate between different types of grain, landrace wheat varieties and einkorn wheat that only contain low levels of pro-inflammatory gluten.

Cruciferous vegetables:
broccoli, kale, pak choi, Brussels sprouts, cauliflower, red cabbage, horseradish, radishes, turnip, watercress.

Leafy green vegetables: spinach, chard, rocket, nettles, dandelions.

Alliums: garlic, spring onions, red onions, yellow onions. These are good sources of inulin. Vary with Jerusalem artichokes or green bananas if you like.

Topping:

Cold-pressed olive oil, rapeseed oil or another fat that's as fresh and little processed as possible, regardless of whether it's animal or plant-based. Avoid hydrogenated fat completely.

Seeds and nuts: walnuts, Brazil nuts, cashew nuts, almonds, hazelnuts, pistachios, macadamia nuts, peanuts (actually a legume), pumpkin seeds, sunflower seeds, sesame seeds, chia seeds.

Mushrooms: porcini, enoki, chanterelles, white and brown mushrooms, shiitake, oyster mushrooms, king trumpet mushrooms, ram's head.

Top tip!

Every day, eat vegetables that contain a wide variety of fibre types.

Every day, eat a little fermented food, such as sauerkraut, kefir or anything containing lactic acid bacteria, or unpasteurised cheese.

Eat all the colours of the rainbow. Make it a habit to include as many colours as possible on your plate. Choose colourful alternatives when you buy food.

Eat tasty, deliciously scented food with a large proportion of aromatic herbs and spices. Encourage growers and shops to offer heritage vegetables with slightly more bitter flavours. Look for farmers' markets or farm shops.

Vary with:

Berries (fresh, dried or frozen): lingonberries, blueberries, blackberries, goji berries, red grapes, strawberries, raspberries, currants, cherries.

Challenge yourself each week by buying at least one vegetable or other ingredient you don't normally eat.

Fruit: apples, bananas, melon, avocados, pineapple, oranges, figs, dates, plums, pomegranate, mangoes, kiwi.

Eat mindfully. Don't eat on the go. Don't do anything else while you're eating. Set down your fork between mouthfuls.

Herbs and spices: turmeric, black pepper, ginger, oregano, basil, mustard powder, thyme, nutmeg, cloves, coriander, cinnamon.

Creamy salsify tagliatelle with mushrooms

Fungi are an ancient part of the Nordic kitchen, which it now turns out are also full of healthy fibre. Salsify, on the other hand, arrived in Sweden in the 1600s, imported by the nobility. In recent years, this relative of the dandelion has become known as poor man's asparagus, thanks to its delicate flavour.

500g mushrooms
1 shallot
300ml cream
2 bay leaves
a pinch of grated nutmeg
1 tablespoon butter
500g salsify
1 lemon
2 tablespoons chopped parsley
2 tablespoons chopped chive
salt and black pepper, freshly
   ground

1. Brush and pick over the mushrooms. Set aside 4–5 mushrooms to serve.
2. Place the remaining mushrooms in a bowl and top up with water. Leave to stand for 15 minutes.
3. Halve the shallot lengthways, keeping the skin on, and place in a saucepan with the cream, bay leaves, nutmeg and a pinch of black pepper.
4. Place the saucepan over the heat, allow to boil and simmer carefully until half of the liquid remains. Sieve and remove the bay leaves.
5. Carefully lift the mushrooms out of the water without stirring the water.
6. Place the mushrooms in a frying pan and allow the liquid to cook off over a high heat.
7. When the pan is dry, add the butter and fry the mushrooms until golden brown.
8. Blend the cream with the fried mushrooms in a food processor until smooth. Season with salt.
9. Peel the salsify with a potato peeler and place in cold water with the juice of the lemon.
10. Bring 3–4 litres of lightly salted water to the boil.
11. Cut tagliatelle-shaped strips off the salsify with the potato peeler.
12. Cook the salsify for 30 seconds in the boiling water.
13. Drain off the water and leave to steam thoroughly.
14. Mix the mushroom cream with the tagliatelle, top with chopped parsley and chives and grate the reserved raw mushrooms over.

Fresh berries, whole rye and honey milk

Boost your immune system with fresh berries and this incredibly tasty honey milk. The whole rye gives you fibre and is nicely chewy. Quite simply a wonderful breakfast!

100g whole rye
300g mixed berries
300ml milk, ideally unpasteurised
2 egg yolks
1 tablespoon honey, ideally
  unpasteurised
small pinch of salt

1. Cook the rye according to the instructions on the packaging, ideally until it's still a little chewy. Cool and rinse with cold water.
2. Pick over the berries.
3. Whisk together the milk, egg yolks, honey and salt. If necessary, season with more salt and honey.
4. Completely drain the cooked rye.
5. Serve the fresh berries with the rye and honey milk.

Epilogue

As you see, the diets that are thought to be best for human health aren't complicated or extreme, but simply normal food based on familiar, traditional foundations. It doesn't need to be any more difficult than that. The key is variation in fibre-rich ingredients, colours and flavours. In brief, food that makes you, your taste buds and your billions of gut bacteria happy and satisfied at the same time.

But we're also at a very clear crossroads where we'd like to defend the importance of food and dining.

The obvious, broad road that leads from here is paved with research money and leads to a vast heap of probiotic medications. Here, we'll learn how our gut flora and our immune system can be stabilised by adding individual bacteria that suit individual people. If we follow this path without looking back, food and medicine will merge together and be increasingly dominated by the pharmaceutical industry.

The other, narrower road gets nowhere near as much research funding and therefore runs the risk of being completely overgrown. But this way leads to re-establishing old plant types with a richer content of antioxidants and other bioactive substances. It also involves defending the biological diversity of our surroundings, which ultimately helps both us and our environment to feel better.

We hope to take the second route. Because this way means that not only you and I and our food will be happier – but that the entire planet will become more harmonious.

Recipes

Tomato salad with homemade
 cream cheese p. 61
Waldorf salad p. 77
Weed salad with olive oil and
 hazelnuts p. 25

Soups
Bone marrow stock p. 220
Raw butternut squash and ginger
 soup p. 28
Roast chicken soup with
 crudités p. 133
Spicy tomato soup with lentils p. 95

Bread
Crispbread with potatoes p. 205
Emmer flour baguette p. 207
Sourdough bread p. 206

Side dishes and snacks
Beansprouts with seeds and
 lentils p. 212
Egg halves with anchovies p. 109
Fresh berries, whole rye and honey
 milk p. 233
Happy Food snack platter p. 39
Mackerel sandwich p. 208
Øllebrød p. 203
Overnight oats with lingonberries
 and milk p. 149
Seasonal greens with
 carrot dip p. 25
Skyr with Nordic berries
 and seeds p. 211
Spiced aubergine p. 57
Tomato dip with sourdough bread
 and olive oil p. 81

Index

Index

Index

Øllebrød (see page 203)

Bibliography

Part 1

Chapter 1: Bottoms up!

Bordenstein, SR et al: Host Biology in Light of the Microbiome: Ten Principles of Holobionts and Hologenomes. PLoS Biol. 2015 Aug 18;13(8):e1002226. doi: 10.1371/journal. pbio.1002226. eCollection 2015 Aug.

El Kaoutari, Abdessamad et al: The abundance and variety of carbohydrate-active enzymes in the human gut microbiota, Nature Reviews Microbiology volume 11, pages 497–504 (2013).

Knight, Rob: Follow your gut - The enormous impact of tiny microbes, 2015.

Chapter 2: Presenting: Your gut flora

Cryan, John & Dinan, Ted: The psychobiotic revolution, 2018.

Cryan, John: föreläsning I Bethesda, juli 2017.

Falony, G et al: Population-level analysis of gut microbiome variation. Science. 2016 Apr 29;352(6285):560-4. doi: 10.1126/science. aad3503. Epub 2016 Apr 28.

Fletcher, Joshua R et al: Shifts in the Gut Metabolome and Clostridium difficile Transcriptome throughout Colonization and Infection in a Mouse Model, mSphere Mar 2018, DOI: 10.1128/mSphere.00089-18.

Chapter 3: One with nature

Haahtela, T.: Allergy is rare where butterflies flourish in a biodiverse environment. Allergy, 64: 1799–1803. doi:10.1111/j.1398-9995.2009.02246.x. 2009.

Prescott, Susan & Logan, Alan: The secret life of your microbiome, 2017.

Prescott, Susan: talk at ISNPR's conference in Washington, July 2017.

Twohig-Bennett, Caoimhe: The health benefits of the great outdoors: A systematic review and meta-analysis of greenspace exposure and health outcomes, Environmental Research, Volume 166, October 2018, Pages 628-637.

WHO: Connecting global priorities: biodiversity and human health: a state of knowledge review, 2015.

Chapter 4: Dizzying new research

Bach, JF et al: The effect of infections on susceptibility to autoimmune and allergic diseases. N Engl J Med. 2002 Sep 19;347(12):911-20.

Blaser, Martin: Missing microbes - How the overuse of antibiotics is fueling our modern plagues, 2014.

Borlée, F et al: Residential proximity to livestock farms is associated with a lower prevalence of atopy, Occup Environ Med Published Online First: 30 April 2018. doi:10.1136/oemed-2017-104769.

Clemente, JC et al: The microbiome of uncontacted Amerindians. Sci Adv. 2015 Apr 3;1(3) pii: e1500183.

Handelsman, Jo: talk at the AAAS conference in Austin Texas, February 2018.

Knight, Rob: interviewed in Austin Texas in February 2018.

Knight, Rob & Gilbert, Jack: Dirt is good - The advantage of germs for your child's developing immune system, 2017.

Martínez, I et al: The gut microbiota of rural Papua New Guineans: Composition, diversity patterns, and ecological processes. Cell Rep. 2015 Apr 28;11(4):527-38. doi: 10.1016/j. celrep.2015.03.049. Epub 2015 Apr 16.

Strachan, DP: Hay fever, hygiene, and household size. BMJ. 1989 Nov 18;299(6710):1259-60.

Chapter 5: What most affects your gut flora?

Atarishi, K et al: Ectopic colonization of oral bacteria in the intestine drives TH1 cell induction and inflammation. Science, 2017. DOI: 10.1126/science.aan4526.

Clarke, SF et al: Exercise and associated dietary extremes impact on gut microbial diversity. Gut. 2014 Dec;63(12):1913-20. doi: 10.1136/gutjnl-2013-306541. Epub 2014 Jun 9.

Collado, MC, Engen PA, Bandín C, et al: Timing of food intake impacts daily rhythms of human salivary microbiota: a randomized, crossover study. FASEB J. 2018. doi: 10.1096/fj.201700697RR.

Dao, MC et al: Akkermansia muciniphila and improved metabolic health during a dietary intervention in obesity: relationship with gut microbiome richness and ecology. Gut. 2016 Mar;65(3):426-36. doi: 10.1136/gutjnl-2014-308778. Epub 2015 Jun 22.

Egervärn, Maria et al: Risk- och nyttoprofil - Interaktioner mellan maten och tarmfloran – en övergripande sammanställning av kunskapsläget, Livsmedelsverket, 2018.

Fei, N et al: An opportunistic pathogen isolated from the gut of an obese human causes obesity in germfree mice. ISME J. 2013 Apr;7(4):880-4. doi: 10.1038/ismej.2012.153. Epub 2012 Dec 13.

Jakubowicz, D et al: Influences of Breakfast on Clock Gene Expression and Postprandial Glycemia in Healthy Individuals and Individuals With Diabetes: A Randomized Clinical Trial, Diabetes Care 40(11):dc162753, August 2017.

Karl, JP et al: Changes in intestinal microbiota composition and metabolism coincide with increased intestinal permeability in young adults under prolonged physiological stress, American Journal of Physiology - Gastrointestinal and Liver Physiology, Volume 312, Issue 6, Juni 2017, Pages G559-G571.

Kato-Kataoka et al: Fermented milk containing Lactobacillus casei strain Shirota prevents the onset of physical symptoms in medical students under academic examination stress Benef. Microbes, 7 (2016), pp. 153-156.

Knowles, SR et al: Investigating the role of perceived stress on bacterial flora activity and salivary cortisol secretion: A possible mechanism underlying susceptibility to illness. Biological psychology, 77, no. 2 (February 2008): 132-37.

Kuno, T et al: Reduction in hepatic secondary bile acids caused by short-term antibiotic-induced dysbiosis decreases mouse serum glucose and triglyceride levels. Sci Rep. 2018 Jan 19;8(1):1253. doi: 10.1038/s41598-018-19545-1.

Lyall, Laura M et al: Association of disrupted circadian rhythmicity with mood disorders, subjective wellbeing, and cognitive function: a cross-sectional study of 91 105 participants from the UK Biobank, The Lancet Psychiatry, Published online 15 May.

Mach, Núria et al: Endurance exercise and gut microbiota - A review, Journal of Sport and Health Science, Volume 6, Issue 2, June 2017, Pages 179-197.

Maier, L et al: Extensive impact of non-antibiotic drugs on human gut bacteria. Nature. 2018 Mar 29;555(7698):623-628. doi: 10.1038/nature25979. Epub 2018 Mar 19.

Maier, TV et al: Impact of Dietary Resistant Starch on the Human Gut Microbiome, Metaproteome, and Metabolome. MBio. 2017 Oct 17;8(5). pii: e01343-17. doi: 10.1128/mBio.01343-17.

Mozaffarian, D et al: Changes in diet and lifestyle and long-term weight gain in women and men. N Engl J Med. 2011 Jun 23;364(25):2392-404. doi: 10.1056/NEJMoa1014296.

Senthong, Vichai et al: Trimethylamine N-Oxide and Mortality Risk in Patients with Peripheral Artery Disease, Journal of the American Heart Association. 2016;5:e004237 Originally published 19 October 2016.

Tramontano, M et al: Nutritional preferences of human gut bacteria reveal their metabolic idiosyncrasies. Nat Microbiol. 2018 Apr;3(4):514-522. doi: 10.1038/s41564-018-0123-9. Epub 2018 Mar 19.

Vandeputte, D et al: Stool consistency is strongly associated with gut microbiota richness and composition, enterotypes and bacterial growth rates. Gut. 2016 Jan;65(1):57-62. doi: 10.1136/gutjnl-2015-309618. Epub 2015 Jun 11.

Wilck, N et al: Salt-responsive gut commensal modulates TH17 axis and disease. Nature. 2017 Nov 30;551(7682):585-589. doi: 10.1038/nature24628. Epub 2017 Nov 15.

Wu, Gary D et al: Linking Long-Term Dietary Patterns with Gut Microbial Enterotypes, Science. 2011 Oct 7; 334(6052): 105-108.

Published online 2011 Sep 1. doi: 10.1126/ science.1208344.

Zhu, W et al; Gut Microbe-Generated Trimethylamine N-Oxide From Dietary Choline Is Prothrombotic in Subjects. Circulation. 2017 Apr 25;135(17):1671-1673. doi: 10.1161/ CIRCULATIONAHA.116.025338.

Chapter 6: Emotional eating

Blitz, J et al: The Risk of Chronic Gastrointestinal Disorders Following Acute Infection with Intestinal Parasites. Front Microbiol. 2018 Jan 23;9:17. doi: 10.3389/fmicb.2018.00017. eCollection 2018.

Clark, William F et al: The Walkerton health study 2002-2008. Final report. Submitted to the Ontario Ministry of Health and Long-Term Care.

Desai, MS et al: A Dietary Fiber-Deprived Gut Microbiota Degrades the Colonic Mucus Barrier and Enhances Pathogen Susceptibility. Cell. 2016 Nov 17;167(5):1339-1353.e21. doi: 10.1016/j. cell.2016.10.043.

Dicksved, J et al; Susceptibility to Campylobacter infection is associated with the species composition of the human fecal microbiota. MBio. 2014 Sep 16;5(5):e01212-14. doi: 10.1128/ mBio.01212-14.

Ennart, Henrik & Nilsson Mats-Eric: Döden i grytan: om vår rädsla för riktig mat, 2010.

Hanevik, K et al: Irritable bowel syndrome and chronic fatigue 6 years after Giardia infection: a controlled prospective cohort study. Clin Infect Dis. 2014 Nov 15;59(10):1394-400. doi: 10.1093/cid/ciu629. Epub 2014 Aug 12.

Litleskare, Sverre et al: Prevalence of Irritable Bowel Syndrome and Chronic Fatigue 10 Years After Giardia Infection, Clinical Gastroenterology and Hepatology, 2018, ISSN 1542-3565.

Marshall, JK et al: Eight year prognosis of postinfectious irritable bowel syndrome following waterborne bacterial dysentery. Gut. 2010 Maj;59(5):605-11.doi: 10.1136/ gut.2009.202234.

Marshall, JK et al: Intestinal permeability in patients with irritable bowel syndrome after a waterborne outbreak of acute gastroenteritis in

Walkerton, Ontario. Aliment Pharmacol Ther. 2004 Dec;20(11-12):1317-22.

Marshall, JK et al: Incidence and epidemiology of irritable bowel syndrome after a large waterborne outbreak of bacterial dysentery. Gastroenterology. 2006 Aug;131(2):445-50; quiz 660.

Shankar, S et al: Dietary and Microbial Oxazoles Induce Intestinal Inflammation by Modulating Aryl Hydrocarbon Receptor Responses, Cell, 2018, Volume 173, Issue 5, 1123 - 1134.e11.

Spiller, R et al: Increased rectal mucosal enteroendocrine cells, T lymphocytes, and increased gut permeability following acute Campylobacter enteritis and in post-dysenteric irritable bowel syndrome, Gut. 2000 Dec; 47(6): 804-811. doi: 10.1136/gut.47.6.804

Thabane, M et al: An outbreak of acute bacterial gastroenteritis is associated with an increased incidence of irritable bowel syndrome in children. Am J Gastroenterol. 2010 Apr;105(4):933-9. doi: 10.1038/ajg.2010.74. Epub 2010 Feb 23.

Verdu, EF et al: Chronic gastrointestinal consequences of acute infectious diarrhea: evolving concepts in epidemiology and pathogenesis. Am J Gastroenterol. 2012 Jul;107(7):981-9. doi: 10.1038/ajg.2012.65. Epub 2012 Apr 17.

Yang, WH et al: Recurrent infection progressively disables host protection against intestinal inflammation. Science. 2017 Oct 22;358(6370). pii: e01343-17. doi: 10.1126/science.aao5610.

Chapter 7: Food and well-being

Arvidsson, L et al: Bidirectional associations between psychosocial well-being and adherence to healthy dietary guidelines in European children: prospective findings from the IDEFICS study. BMC Public Health. 2017 Dec 14;17(1):926. doi: 10.1186/s12889-017-4920-5.

Bercik, P et al: The anxiolytic effect of Bifidobacterium longum NCC3001 involves vagal pathways for gut-brain communication. Neurogastroenterol Motil. 2011 Dec;23(12):1132-9. doi: 10.1111/j.1365-2982.2011.01796.x. Epub 2011 Oct 11.

Burokas, A et al: Targeting the Microbiota-Gut-Brain Axis: Prebiotics Have Anxiolytic and

Antidepressant-like Effects and Reverse the Impact of Chronic Stress in Mice. Biol Psychiatry. 2017 Oct 1;82(7):472-487. doi: 10.1016/j.biopsych.2016.12.031. Epub 2017 Feb 24.

Gangwisch, JE et al: High glycemic index diet as a risk factor for depression: analyses from the Women's Health Initiative. Am J Clin Nutr. 2015 Aug;102(2):454-63. doi: 10.3945/ajcn.114.103846. Epub 2015 Jun 24.

Hetrick, SE et al: Newer generation antidepressants for depressive disorders in children and adolescents. Cochrane Database Syst Rev. 2012 Nov 14;11:CD004851. doi: 10.1002/14651858.CD004851.pub3.

Jacka, FN et al: Western diet is associated with a smaller hippocampus: a longitudinal investigation. BMC Med. 2015 Sep 8;13:215. doi: 10.1186/s12916-015-0461-x.

Jacka, FN et al: A randomised controlled trial of dietary improvement for adults with major depression (the 'SMILES' trial). BMC Med. 2017 Jan 30;15(1):23. doi: 10.1186/s12916-017-0791-y.

Jacka, FN et al: Association of Western and traditional diets with depression and anxiety in women. Am J Psychiatry. 2010 Mar;167(3):305-11. doi: 10.1176/appi.ajp.2009.09060881. Epub 2010 Jan 4.

Jacka, FN et al: The association between habitual diet quality and the common mental disorders in community-dwelling adults: the Hordaland Health study. Psychosom Med. 2011 Jul-Aug;73(6):483-90. doi: 10.1097/PSY.0b013e318222831a. Epub 2011 Jun 28.

Jakobsen, JC et al: Selective serotonin reuptake inhibitors versus placebo in patients with major depressive disorder. A systematic review with meta-analysis and Trial Sequential Analysis. BMC Psychiatry. 2017 Feb 8;17(1):58. doi: 10.1186/s12888-016-1173-2.

Kalliomäki, M et al: Probiotics in primary prevention of atopic disease: a randomised placebo-controlled trial. Lancet. 2001 Apr 7;357(9262):1076-9.

Koloski, NA et al: The brain–gut pathway in functional gastrointestinal disorders is bidirectional: a 12-year prospective population-based study, Gut 2012;61:1284-1290.

Li, Y et al: Dietary patterns and depression risk: A meta-analysis. Psychiatry Res. 2017 Jul;253:373-382. doi: 10.1016/j.psychres.2017.04.020. Epub 2017 Apr 11. Review.

Lucas, M et al: Inflammatory dietary pattern and risk of depression among women. Brain Behav Immun. 2014 Feb;36:46-53. doi: 10.1016/j.bbi.2013.09.014. Epub 2013 Oct 1.

Molendijk, M et al: Diet quality and depression risk: A systematic review and dose-response meta-analysis of prospective studies. J Affect Disord. 2018 Jan 15;226:346-354. doi: 10.1016/j.jad.2017.09.022. Epub 2017 Sep 23.

Mozaffarian, D et al: Dietary guidelines and health – is nutrition science up to the task? BMJ. 2018 Mar 16;360:k822. doi: 10.1136/bmj.k822.

Naseribafrouei, A. et al: Correlation Between the Human Fecal Microbiota and Depression, Neurogastroenterology and Motility: The Official Journal of the European Gastrointestinal Motility Society 26, no. 8 (August 2014): 1155–62.

Parletta, N et al: A Mediterranean-style dietary intervention supplemented with fish oil improves diet quality and mental health in people with depression: A randomized controlled trial (HELFIMED). Nutr Neurosci. 2017 Dec 7:1-14. doi: 10.1080/1028415X.2017.1411320

Rachelle, S. Opie et al: A modified Mediterranean dietary intervention for adults with major depression: Dietary protocol and feasibility data from the SMILES trial, Nutritional Neuroscience, Published online: 19 Apr 2017.

Reichenberg, A et al: Cytokine-associated emotional and cognitive disturbances in humans. Arch Gen Psychiatry. 2001 May;58(5):445-52.

Rook, GA et al: Microbiota, Immunoregulatory Old Friends and Psychiatric Disorders, Advances in Experimental Medicine and Biology 817 (2014): 319-56.

Rook, Graham et al: Evolution, human-microbe interactions, and life history plasticity, The Lancet, Volume 390, Issue 10093 , 521–530.

Sánchez-Villegas, A et al: Association of the Mediterranean dietary pattern with the incidence of depression: the Seguimiento Universidad de Navarra/University of Navarra follow-up (SUN) cohort. Arch Gen Psychiatry. 2009 Oct;66(10):1090-8. doi: 10.1001/archgenpsychiatry.2009.129.

Sánchez-Villegas, A et al: Mediterranean dietary pattern and depression: the PREDIMED randomized trial, BMC Med. 2013; 11: 208. Published online 2013 Sep 20. doi: 10.1186/1741-7015-11-208.

Sarris, J et al: International Society for Nutritional Psychiatry Research consensus position statement: nutritional medicine in modern psychiatry. World Psychiatry. 2015 Oct;14(3):370-1. doi: 10.1002/wps.20223.

Schuppner, R et al: Neurological Sequelae in Adults After E coli O104: H4 Infection-Induced Hemolytic-Uremic Syndrome. Medicine (Baltimore). 2016 Feb;95(6):e2337. doi: 10.1097/MD.0000000000002337.

Tabung, FK et al: The association between dietary inflammatory index and risk of colorectal cancer among postmenopausal women: results from the Women's Health Initiative. Cancer Causes Control. 2015 Mar;26(3):399-408. doi: 10.1007/s10552-014-0515-y. Epub 2014 Dec 31.

Part 2

Chapter 8: Set for success

Nilsson, Mats-Eric: Måltidens magi - om matbordets hotade gemenskap, 2017.

Perofsky, AC et al: Hierarchical social networks shape gut microbial composition in wild Verreaux's sifaka. Proc Biol Sci. 2017 Dec 6;284(1868). pii: 20172274. doi: 10.1098/rspb.2017.2274.

Pollan, Michael: Cooked - a natural history of transformation, 2014.

Wrangham, Richard: Catching fire - How cooking made us human, 2009.

Chapter 9: How do you really eat?

Stahl, B & Goldstein, E: A mindfulness-based stress reduction workbook, 2010.

Warren, JM et al: A structured literature review on the role of mindfulness, mindful eating and intuitive eating in changing eating behaviours: effectiveness and associated potential mechanisms. Nutr Res Rev. 2017 Dec;30(2):272-283. doi: 10.1017/S0954422417000154. Epub 2017 Jul 18.

Winkens, LHH et al: Associations of mindful eating domains with depressive symptoms and depression in three European countries. J Affect Disord. 2018 Mar 1;228:26-32. doi: 10.1016/j.jad.2017.11.069. Epub 2017 Nov 14.

Winkens, LHH et al: The Mindful Eating Behavior Scale: Development and Psychometric Properties in a Sample of Dutch Adults Aged 55 Years and Older. J Acad Nutr Diet. 2018 Apr 11. pii: S2212-2672(18)30145-X. doi: 10.1016/j.jand.2018.01.015.

Chapter 10: Flavours for both big and small

Bian, G et al: The Gut Microbiota of Healthy Aged Chinese is Similar to That of the Healthy Young. mSphere. 2017 Sep 27;2(5). pii: e00327-17. doi: 10.1128/mSphere.00327-17. eCollection 2017 Sep-Oct.

Kumar, M et al: Human gut microbiota and healthy aging: Recent developments and future prospective. Nutr Healthy Aging. 2016 Oct 27;4(1):3-16. doi: 10.3233/NHA-150002.

Pechal, JL et al: A large-scale survey of the postmortem human microbiome, and its potential to provide insight into the living health condition. Sci Rep. 2018 Apr 10;8(1):5724. doi: 10.1038/s41598-018-23989-w.

Chapter 11: Emotional upsets

Bègue, L et al: Omega-3 supplements reduce self-reported physical aggression in healthy adults. Psychiatry Res. 2018 Mar;261:307-311. doi: 10.1016/j.psychres.2017.12.038. Epub 2017 Dec 15.

Gesch, B: Adolescence: Does good nutrition = good behaviour? Nutr Health. 2013 Jan;22(1):55-65. Epub 2014 Feb 4.

Gesch, CB: Influence of supplementary vitamins, minerals and essential fatty acids on the antisocial behaviour of young adult prisoners. Randomised, placebo-controlled trial. Br J Psychiatry. 2002 Jul;181:22-8.

Zaalberg, A et al: Effects of nutritional supplements on aggression, rule-breaking, and psychopathology among young adult prisoners.

Aggress Behav. 2010 Mar-Apr;36(2): 117-26. doi: 10.1002/ab.20335.

Chapter 12: We're all different

Zeevi, D et al: Personalized Nutrition by Prediction of Glycemic Responses. Cell. 2015 Nov 19;163(5):1079-1094. doi: 10.1016/j.cell.2015.11.001.

Chapter 13: A Nordic breeze is blowing

Anderson, JJ et al: Diet Quality -The Greeks Had It Right! Nutrients. 2016 Oct 14;8(10). pii: E636.

Dahiya, Sonia: Role of phytate and phytases in human nutrition, International Journal of Food Science and Nutrition ISSN: 2455-4898 www.foodsciencejournal.com Volume 1; Issue 1; January 2016; Page No. 39-42.

DiGirolamo, Ann M et al: Role of zinc in maternal and child mental health, The American Journal of Clinical Nutrition, Volume 89, Issue 3, 1 March 2009, Pages 940S–945S, https://doi.org/10.3945/ajcn.2008.26692C.

Ford, CT et al: Identification of (poly)phenol treatments that modulate the release of pro-inflammatory cytokines by human lymphocytes. Br J Nutr. 2016 May 28;115(10):1699-710. doi: 10.1017/S0007114516000805. Epub 2016 Mar 17.

Gupta, Raj Kishor et al: Reduction of phytic acid and enhancement of bioavailable micronutrients in food grains, J Food Sci Technol. 2015 Feb; 52(2): 676-684. Published online 2013 Apr 24. doi: 10.1007/s13197-013-0978-y.

Healey, G et al: Habitual dietary fibre intake influences gut microbiota response to an inulin-type fructanprebiotic: a randomised, double-blind, placebo-controlled, cross-over, human intervention study. Br J Nutr. 2018 Jan;119(2):176-189. doi: 10.1017/S0007114517003440. Epub 2018 Jan 8.

Hellsten, Alies: Vete då och nu: Släktskap och mineralkoncentration, Institutionen för molekylära vetenskaper, SLU, 2017:18 Uppsala, 2017.

Harach, T et al: Reduction of Abeta amyloid pathology in APPPS1 transgenic mice in the absence of gut microbiota. Sci Rep. 2017 Feb 8;7:41802. doi: 10.1038/srep41802. Erratum in: Sci Rep. 2017 Jul 10;7:46856.

Johansson, EV et al: Effects of indigestible carbohydrates in barley on glucose metabolism appetite and voluntary food intake over 16 h in healthy adults, Nutr J. 2013 Apr 11;12:46. doi: 10.1186/147528911246.

Li, Z et al: Dietary zinc and iron intake and risk of depression: A meta-analysis. Psychiatry Res. 2017 May;251:41-47. doi: 10.1016/j.psychres.2017.02.006. Epub 2017 Feb 3.

Prykhodko, Olena et al: Impact of Rye Kernel-Based Evening Meal on Microbiota Composition of Young Healthy Lean Volunteers With an Emphasis on Their Hormonal and Appetite Regulations, and Blood Levels of Brain-Derived Neurotrophic Factor, Front. Nutr. | doi: 10.3389/fnut.2018.00045.

The 2015 European Union report on pesticide residues in food, EFSA Journal: 11 April 2017.

Zhao, Liping et al: Gut bacteria selectively promoted by dietary fibers alleviate type 2 diabetes, Science 09 Mar 2018: Vol. 359, Issue 6380, pp. 1151-1156 DOI: 10.1126/science.aao5774.

Chapter 14: Back to your roots

Ferrão, J et al: Impact of Mushroom Nutrition on Microbiota and Potential for Preventative Health. Journal of Food and Nutrition Research, vol. 5, no. 4 (2017): 226-233. doi: 10.12691/jfnr-5-4-4.

Kalaras, MD et al: Mushrooms: A rich source of the antioxidants ergothioneine and glutathione. Food Chem. 2017 Oct 15;233:429-433. doi: 10.1016/j.foodchem.2017.04.109. Epub 2017 Apr 20.

Sari, Miriam et al: Screening of beta-glucan contents in commercially cultivated and wild growing mushrooms, Food Chemistry 216 (2017) 45–51.

BLOOMSBURY ABSOLUTE
Bloomsbury Publishing Plc
50 Bedford Square, London,
WC1B 3DP, UK

BLOOMSBURY, BLOOMSBURY
ABSOLUTE, the Diana logo and the
Absolute Press logo are trademarks
of Bloomsbury Publishing Plc

First published in 2018 by
Bookmark Förlag, Sweden.

Published by arrangement with
Nordin Agency, AB, Sweden

First published in Great Britain
2020.

Text © Niklas Ekstedt and Henrik
Ennart, 2018
Photography © David Loftus, 2018
Illustrations and design © Katy
Kimbell, 2018

Translated by Quarto Translations,
2019

A catalogue record for this book is
available from the British Library.

ISBN
HB: 9781472974723
ePUB: 9781472974730
ePDF: 9781472974747

2 4 6 8 10 9 7 5 3 1

Printed and bound in China by
Toppan Leefung Printing Ltd

Bloomsbury Publishing Plc makes
every effort to ensure that the
papers used in the manufacture of
our books are natural, recyclable
products made from wood grown
in well-managed forests. Our
manufacturing processes conform to
the environmental regulations of the
country of origin.

To find out more about our authors
and books visit www.bloomsbury.
com and sign up for our newsletters.